SERIES EDITOR: LEE JOHNSON

OSPREY MILITARY MEN-AT-ARMS

LOUIS XV's ARMY (2) FRENCH INFANTRY

TEXT BY
RENÉ CHARTRAND

COLOUR PLATES BY
EUGÈNE LELIÈPVRE

OSPREY
MILITARY

First published in Great Britain in 1996 by OSPREY, a division of Reed Consumer Books Ltd. Michelin House, 81 Fulham Road, London SW3 6RB
and Auckland, Melbourne, Singapore and Toronto

© Copyright 1996 Reed International Books Ltd.

All rights reserved. Apart from any fair dealing for the purpose of private study, research, criticism or review, as permitted under the Copyright, Designs and Patents Act, 1988, no part of this publication may be reproduced, stored in a retrieval system, or transmitted in any form or by any means, electronic, electrical, chemical, mechanical, optical, photocopying, recording or otherwise, without the prior permission of the copyright owner. Enquiries should be addressed to the Publishers.

OSPREY
2nd Floor, Unit 6, Spring Gardens Tinworth Street Vauxhall, London SE11 5EH

ISBN 1 85532 625 6

Filmset in Singapore by Pica Ltd.
Printed through World Print Ltd, Hong Kong

Edited by: Sharon van der Merwe
Design: Alan Hamp

For a catalogue of all books published by Osprey Military please write to:
The Marketing Manager, Osprey Publishing Ltd., Michelin House,
81 Fulham Road, London SW3 6RB

Author's Note

This book is the second in a series of five devoted to the organisation, uniforms and weapons of the largest military force in 18th-century western Europe: Louis XV's French army. This volume examines the 'French' infantry, that is to say, the units of the land army recruited from men born in metropolitan France. These troops included part of the royal guard, most regiments of the line infantry, independent garrison companies and the royal militia. Special emphasis has been given to metropolitan regiments serving overseas, since they were nearly always pitted against British or colonial American forces.

Subsequent volumes will cover: the foreign infantry of the guard and of the line; the artillery; the light troops, including hussars and legions; and auxiliary corps such as engineers, staff officers and local militias. The final volume will examine the colonial troops and militias in New France, the West Indies, Africa and India, as well as marines and other naval troops based in France. All will be illustrated with contemporary illustrations and portraits, and some 40 colour plates, each with several figures. When completed, it is hoped this collection of volumes will form the most complete account on the organisation and material culture of Louis XV's army published for a century.

Artist's Note

Readers may care to note that the original paintings from which the colour plates in this book were prepared are available for private sale. All reproduction copyright whatsoever is retained by the Publisher. All enquiries should be addressed to:
M. Eugène Lelièpvre, 33 rue Boileau, 92120 Montrouge, France

The Publishers regret that they can enter into no correspondence upon this matter.

LOUIS XV's ARMY (2) FRENCH INFANTRY

INTRODUCTION

In Louis XV's army the classification of 'French' infantry denoted troops recruited from men born and raised in France. These regiments were called, naturally enough, *infanterie française* as opposed to the mercenary 'foreign' infantry recruited elsewhere from other nationalities. In the French infantry, which made up the bulk of the army, all officers and men were to be of the Roman Catholic faith, the official state religion.

Regimental recruiting parties went to towns and villages looking for likely young volunteers, inducing them to enlist with the usual promises – quick money, fast women, good wines and great glory. The enlistment period was for six or eight years but release from service might not be respected if the unit was short of men.

Many regiments were identified with the province that was its particular, but not exclusive, recruiting area. Similarly, regiments raised by a gentleman tended to include a core of enlisted men from their colonel's fiefdom and its surrounding areas. Thus up to half of the men in a regiment might be from the same province; but many others would have been from all over the realm. They were often recruited in Paris, usually near the Pont-Neuf, where the recruiting parties hung about.

Officers of line infantry regiments were generally from a fairly humble background. Most came from provincial noble families which, as brave and loyal as they were, had little money or influence. Serving as officers in the army was their one chance to gain some glory – and a decent pension if they lived to retire. They tended to take the view that army commissions were their birthright and felt that '*roturiers*' (non-noble) officers, however worthy and brave, were not 'in their rightful place' in society.

Up to the mid-18th century about a third of the officers were *roturiers*. This decreased thereafter: from 1750 many officers were admitted to the nobility for their long and distinguished services. Opposition to commissioning *roturiers* grew during and after the Seven Years War, and the nobles finally won their point in a 'battle' that spanned Louis XV's reign. The long-term effect was to dash hopes for advancement and relegate soldiers of exceptional talent to the lower ranks which, in time, had disastrous consequences for the nobility in the next reign.

Louis XV in 1746. This portrait by Maurice-Quentin de La Tour is one of the finest depictions of the king, at a time when he was campaigning in Flanders with his armies. He took the field in 1744, and was present at Fontenoy in 1745 and at Lawfeld, his last battlefield appearance, in 1747.

THE ROYAL GUARD INFANTRY

The royal guard comprised, besides its numerous mounted units, a sizeable number of infantrymen. Nearly all were grouped into the regiments of French and Swiss guards. These regiments were like infantry divisions because of their numerous battalions and the high numbers of soldiers in each company. The remaining units, such as the Gardes de la Porte, were small palace units.

Gardes de la Porte

(Guards of the Gate.) The Gardes de la Porte were possibly the oldest of all guard formations, being 'almost as ancient as the monarchy', according to chevalier de Guignard's history. In Louis XV's reign it consisted of a company of 50 men serving on foot, with five officers whose duty it was to watch the main gates of the king's quarters from six in the morning to six in the evening; the night guard was taken up by the Gardes du Corps.

Their uniform consisted of a blue coat lined and cuffed with red, laced profusely with mixed silver and gold, red waistcoat, breeches and stockings, a black hat with silver and gold lace, and a white cockade. The bandoleer was covered with checked gold and silver lace. The guardsmen were armed with swords and carbines. Officers, at least in the 1720s, wore the same colours but with silver lace edging the coat, which also had silver and gold embroidery. They also had a hat with white plumes and silver embroidered border and a gold-hilted sword.

Gardes-Françaises

(The French Guards.) This was the guard infantry regiment recruited from native-born soldiers – hence its name. It was raised in 1563 and by the 18th century consisted of 32 companies of 200 men each in wartime, divided into up to six battalions. Of these companies, two were of grenadiers formed in 1689; a third company of grenadiers was added in 1719. The regiment saw much action during the reign of Louis XV.

The Gardes-Françaises wore a blue coat with red lining, cuffs, waistcoat, breeches and stockings, white metal buttons and white pointed lace set in threes. Grenadiers had a red cap trimmed with fur, which evolved into a bearskin cap. This basic uniform remained much the same during Louis XV's reign, although the style changed over time.[1]

Gaiters appeared in the 1730s, and from 1743 were required to be white in summer and black in winter. From the 1740s the skirts of the coat were turned back to show the red lining. From 1763 there was blue lining and buttonholes were evenly spaced in front of the coat. The men's accoutrements were buff, edged with white leather. The cartridge box was of reddish brown Russia leather

Garde de la Porte, private, c.1750. (Anne S.K. Brown Military Collection, Brown University, Providence, USA)

Private, Gardes-Françaises Regiment, c.1720. The uniform styles at this time were still reminiscent of Louis XIV's reign. (Print after Delaistre)

---

[1] Apparently in the 1730s there was a proposed dress which included mitre caps and lapels, but this Britannico-Germanic dress was not adopted.

stamped with the royal arms, highlighted by a silver wash. Sergeants were to wear the same uniform as the men but trimmed with silver lace and with a silver lace edging the coat cuffs and pocket flaps. They had silver-edged buff belts and were armed with halberds and silver-hilted swords.

The drummers and fifers of the Gardes-Françaises wore the king's livery: blue coat with red cuffs and lining, garnished with the king's 'great' livery lace and silver lace; red waistcoat, breeches and stockings; and silver-laced hat.

Officers wore the regimental blue coat cuffed and lined with red and had broad silver lace on all seams, and silver buttons; they wore a red waistcoat with silver lace and buttons; red breeches and red (later white) stockings and gaiters. The hats were laced with silver and had white plumes. There was also an undress uniform consisting of blue coats with red cuffs and lining with silver lace and buttons. They were armed with a silver-hilted sword and a spontoon, and on duty they wore a gilt gorget. Only grenadier officers were armed with muskets and bayonets.

Gardes de la Porte de Monsieur

(Guards of the Gate of Monsieur.) Louis XV authorised a personal palace guard for his grandson, Monsieur le Comte de Provence. The Gardes de la Porte de Monsieur were raised in 1772, consisting of four officers and 25 men. They wore a red coat with blue collar, cuffs and lining, a blue waistcoat, red breeches and stockings, and had gold lace and buttons. Arms consisted of halberds and swords. They were disbanded in 1788.

The Line Infantry

The number of regiments, battalions, officers and men could vary greatly. The peacetime establishment of the *infanterie française* in 1740 was 98 regiments totalling 155 battalions: 79,050 NCOs and privates led by 6,300 officers. By 1747 the country was deep into the War of Austrian Succession, and while the French infantry still had 98 regiments, the number of battalions had shot up to 227, mustering 164,318 NCOs and men led by 9,323 officers. A few years later, in 1750, France was at peace, and the army was reduced to 84 regiments having 172 battalions, 88,695 NCOs and men and 5,200 officers. With the Seven Years War, in 1762, this rose to 88 regiments, 187 battalions and 110,000 NCOs and men led by 7,737 officers. Following the Duke of Choiseul's reforms it fell to 66 regiments and 165 battalions; 89,516 NCOs and men with 5,788 officers.

Senior regiments had more than one battalion, but most – 68 out of 98 in 1740 – had a single battalion. Until 1718 each battalion had 15 companies, 14 of fusiliers and one of grenadiers; this was then reduced to nine companies including one of grenadiers. This was raised again to 15 companies in 1734, then dropped to 13 companies from 1749. In 1756 the number of companies was raised to 17 per battalion.[2]

Another innovation, introduced in January 1757, was the issue to each battalion going on campaign in Europe of a light-calibre 'Swedish-style' cannon with limber and three horses. A sergeant and 16 men were

Back view of a private of the Gardes-Françaises Regiment, 1725. Note the appearance of a strap on the coat's left shoulder for the narrow powder flask sling. (Print after J. Pocquet. Anne S.K. Brown Military Collection, Brown University)

---

[2] The battalions sent to New France in 1755 and 1756 were not augmented and remained at 13 companies. The 2nd and 3rd battalions of Berry which landed at Quebec in 1757 only had nine companies each. However, the 2nd battalion of Cambis sent to Louisbourg in 1758 had the full complement of 17 companies having 40 officers, 685 NCOs and privates.

Lock detail of the 1717 Model army musket. Note the distinctive bridle connecting the frizzen spring screw with the frizzen screw. The only known mint example is at the Tower of London. Another was at Dresden but vanished during the Second World War. (Photo courtesy C. Ariès, Nantes)

BELOW 1728 Model army musket. This example has the steel ramrod that replaced wooden ramrods from 1741. (Quebec Fortifications National Historic Site, Quebec City)

detached from the battalion to serve the gun, which was returned to the royal magazines at the end of the campaign. An unofficial temporary company was also formed by drawing good men from other companies. It was usually called the '*Piquet*', although some regiments in Germany started calling it '*Chasseurs*' during the Seven Years War. In May 1760 Marshal Broglie even ordered each regiment in his army to form a chasseur company of 50 men. With the war's end, these unofficial chasseur companies vanished and the number of companies went down to nine per battalion (including one of grenadiers).

For most of Louis XV's reign infantry companies were generally 40 strong for fusiliers and 45 for grenadiers. Each fusilier company had a captain, a lieutenant, two sergeants, three corporals, three *anspessades* (lance-corporals), one drummer and the fusilier privates. Grenadier companies were the same but with the addition of a second lieutenant. Battalion staff included a lieutenant-colonel (named a 'battalion commander' for 2nd, 3rd, etc battalions), a major, an aide-major and two ensigns (to carry colours). Regimental staff usually included a colonel, a surgeon, a sergeant-major, a drum-major and a chaplain. From 1763 fusilier companies were larger, having three officers and 55 NCOs and men; grenadiers had 52.

UNIFORMS

In 1715, at the beginning of Louis XV's long reign, the uniforms worn by the French infantry were very much in the heavy, formal style of the previous reign. The wide-brimmed tricorns for the men were laced with 'false' gold or 'false' silver (mixtures of metallic and silky thread). The cockades were either black or white – it seems there were no set rules; a few, such as the Régiment du Roi, had cockades of white and another colour. In 1767 white for all was finally ordered. The grey-white cloth coats had variously coloured cuffs and lining and many buttons down the front, and the long waistcoats, breeches and stockings were often of colourful hues. Very few regiments had coats with laced buttonholes, but many corps would lace the waistcoats. Many regiments had coat pockets – cut in a variety of ways – and these remained corps distinctions right up to the end of the Seven Years War.

A more debonair spirit and fashion was apparent from the mid 1720s. Hats were worn in a somewhat jaunty way, coats had fewer buttons – they often went just from the neck to below the waist, and cuffs began to get smaller. Gaiters, which had been of utilitarian type, of grey linen used in the field, were now bleached white and became smarter-looking – they were often worn on parade. Cravats, which had been white, were now increasingly of black material and worn somewhat loosely; by the early 1730s they were often tied in large bows.

The royal order of 20 April 1736 streamlined and simplified considerably the dress of the French infantry. The grey-white coat was henceforth to have grey-white lining, with folds only at the sides; the cuffs were to be 'boot' style and 'half as large as usual, with open buttonholes, so that they can be unfolded' over the hand; and the buttons in front were only to go down 'to the level of the pockets' and not lower. The coats were single-breasted with nine to 12 buttons in front. Only the coat cuffs were to 'continue to have the colours affected to each regiment'. The waistcoats were ordered to be shorter and strictly grey-white lined with grey-white, and of no other colour, 'no matter what pretext'. The waistcoat also had buttons going down to below the waist, and were to be plain, without any edging or buttonhole lace. They were not to have pockets or pocket flaps either, but this directive was largely ignored. The breeches were grey-white. Instead of stockings, each corporal, *anspessade*, private soldier and drummer was issued a pair of white linen gaiters.

The 1736 order had specified a practical, less expensive uniform, but regimental distinctions were too muted; many regiments obviously grumbled, and some even adopted coloured waistcoats. The authorities relented. By the order of 19 January 1747 the waistcoats were again allowed to be 'coloured' and to have pockets and pocket flaps, though still no pocket buttons. In the regimental descriptions given below, the coloured waistcoats are generally reported in the 1753 register but they were probably being worn by many as early as 1748.

Coloured collars also became prevalent in many units at that time. Otherwise, the uniforms remained basically the same as ordered in 1736. During the Seven Years War, especially after 1760, a few regiments adopted lapels. This was tolerated as long as the waistcoats were grey-

BELOW Drum case of the Gardes-Françaises, c.1740. In the guard units the royal arms were usually shown with double shields, that of France, with the three gold lilies on blue, and the red with gold chains of Navarre. (Fort Ticonderoga Museum, Ticonderoga, USA)

BELOW, RIGHT Side view, drum case of the Gardes-Françaises, c.1740. The regimental flags, a blue field strewn with gold lilies and a white cross with a crown at each end, form part of the ornaments. (Fort Ticonderoga Museum)

white, so as not to raise the cost of the uniform. A few also sported coloured breeches and buttonholes, no doubt at regimental expense.

Officially, French grenadiers had tricorns like the rest of the men, but bearskin caps became increasingly popular during the 1750s – some army registers begin to mention them and they appear more and more in artwork. British traditions and battle accounts also mention plucking plumes from headgear at Quebec and in Germany; it must have been from bearskin caps, since tricorns had no plumes. Although some regiments had bearskin caps for their grenadiers, most probably went on with the tricorn. These early caps were plain or with a plate in front and a bag behind.

In 1715 rank badges for NCOs were somewhat ill defined officially. In most cases sergeants had real gold lace on their hats and their coat cuffs and their uniform was of better quality cloth than the men's. The corporals and lance-corporals had wool lace on the cuffs. In some regiments the lace edged the cuffs; in others it was applied to the cuff buttonholes. In 1747 it was specified that corporals would have three laced cuff buttonholes and lance-corporals would have the cuff edged only.

Enlisted men were issued a coat and a waistcoat every three years, with a third of the regiment receiving them each year. Hats were issued every second year and breeches annually. The annual necessaries included three shirts, two cravats, two pairs of shoes, three pairs of gaiters, two pairs of stockings and drawers. Small changes, such as the addition of collars of a new colour to the regimental uniform, would be done immediately by company tailors, but sweeping changes would take up to three years to complete. Immediate change of everything meant considerable expense to officers, who were often just a step ahead of their creditors.

Officers were strongly encouraged by Louis XIV to wear regimental uniforms, although they were never actually ordered to do so. In spite of well-publicised protests by officers, the great majority of them had and wore uniforms of better material, usually embellished with plumes and gold or silver lacing.

Fontenoy (11 May 1745) was the site of the famous incident when the 5th and 6th battalions of the Gardes-Françaises faced the British Foot Guards 50 paces away. After much saluting, the polite question of who should shoot first to start the battle was finally settled by a French officer who, in a grand gesture of the 'lace wars', said: 'Après vous, messieurs les Anglais!' (After you!). The British volley hit over 400 officers and men of the Gardes-Françaises. Later, some of the survivors rallied and were among the first to break the British columns which brought victory to the French. (Print after the painting by Philipoteaux)

Louis XV went a step further. By a royal order of 10 March 1729, officers were henceforth ordered to procure themselves regimental uniforms at their cost and to wear them on duty. These uniforms were to be of better material, with gold or silver buttons and hat lace but without any lace on the coat; lacing was allowed on the waistcoat. Finally, in 1737, they were ordered to wear uniforms at all times with their troops. On duty the officers wore a gilded gorget. This was usually plain, until the middle of the 18th century, when a silver badge, usually featuring the crowned arms of France, was added at the centre.

Weapons carried by privates and corporals were a flintlock musket with sling, and bayonet, and a fairly crude straight-bladed sword with a brass hilt. At the beginning of Louis XV's reign muskets and bayonets were of no precisely set model but were to be of 16.7mm calibre. Surviving examples and illustrations show the muskets to have been fairly plain and sturdy weapons, usually with steel furnishings and the barrel fastened to the stock by pins. The bayonets varied: some had a long branch with a short blade.

In 1717 an official model was imposed which had the addition of a leather sling held by a steel barrel band and a swivel screwed into the stock. The bayonet had a long triangular blade with no branch.

In 1728 came a new and most innovative model for its day, lighter and fixed with steel barrel bands which made it much easier to repair and clean. This musket, with various improvements such as steel ramrods from 1741 and improved lock from 1746, was used widely until the 1760s. A 1754 model, whose main new feature was that the sling attachments were underneath, was also manufactured, but in fewer numbers and it does not seem to have been used overseas. The 1763 model, and especially the corrected, lighter version of it in 1766, became the standard weapon into Louis XVI's reign.

The sword, a fairly useless weapon for the 18th-century infantryman, was supposed to be carried until 20 March 1764; then it was officially abolished for privates, but continued to be carried by corporals and sergeants. This attachment to the sword was because in the France of the old regime, the sword was only allowed to be worn by gentlemen, nobles, royal officials and the military. It was a status symbol, and to young peasants one of the attractions of becoming a soldier. Grenadiers carried sabres of various sorts until 1767, when a short sabre model with a slightly curved blade was ordered for all line infantry corporals, sergeants and grenadiers.

Ammunition was carried from the beginning of the 18th century, in a ventral cartridge box which held nine or ten rounds and was covered with a brownish red leather flap. It had a powder horn that held about a pound (say 450mg) of powder and had brass fittings. A buff waistbelt with a brass open buckle held the cartridge box, the sword and bayonet scabbards. The powder horn was carried over the shoulder by a narrow buff sling.

In 1736 the equipment changed to a larger cartridge box, holding 19 rounds, and a small powder flask of leather-covered wood with a wooden stopper tied to it. This was carried over the shoulder by a buff belt. It could be of reddish brown or black leather, with the flap either engraved or stamped with the king's arms or left plain. This cartridge box with a sling was soon termed a '*giberne*', and proved a success: it was maintained

Private, Gardes-Françaises Regiment, 1750s. This side view shows clearly the cartridge box. The flap of guard or line infantry cartridge boxes could be stamped with the royal arms or left plain as shown here. (Print after Eisen. Anne S.K. Brown Military Collection, Brown University)

in the 1747 order. However, 30-round boxes became increasingly more common and seem to have been in general use in the 1750s. In 1767 it was officially changed to a black leather box with a brass badge bearing the king's arms on the flap. From the later 1750s a growing number of regiments whitened their belts, a feature that became official after the Seven Years War.

Sergeants were armed with a sword and a halberd, officers with a sword and spontoon. Officers and sergeants had polearms until 1758, when they were ordered to carry muskets, bayonets and cartridge boxes instead.

INFANTRY REGIMENTS, 1720–1763

The list below attempts to describe the main changes in uniforms which occurred in each infantry regiment. During most of Louis XV's reign regiments were known either by the name of a province or by the name of their colonel. Many were 'gentlemen's regiments' whose name changed with each new colonel – a system that lasted until December 1762, when all gentlemen's regiments were abolished or given the name of a province.

Although French infantry regiments were numbered, it was for precedence, which frequently changed, rather than unit identification as in the British Army. I have used the 1740 and 1758 registers as my main guides for precedence.

The uniform descriptions are given from their earliest fairly complete sources in the 1720s and 1730s, with changes chronicled up to the 1760s from the official army registers. For the sake of clarity the basic description is given again for 1758.[3] Generally, the coat cuffs and pockets each had three buttons and the pocket flaps horizontal, unless otherwise indicated.

Picardie: Grey-white coat, cuffs (four buttons), lining, breeches and stockings, red waistcoat, brass buttons, gold hat lace, and double vertical pockets, each with nine buttons set in threes. From 1736: grey-white waistcoat, white gaiters. 1753: red waistcoat. 1758: grey-white coat, cuffs (four buttons), lining and breeches, red waistcoat, brass buttons, gold hat lace, double vertical pockets, each with nine buttons set in threes.

Champagne: Grey-white coat, cuffs (four buttons), lining, breeches and stockings, red waistcoat, brass buttons, gold hat lace,

Grenadier and fusilier, Gardes-Françaises Regiment, 1760. (Royal Library, Madrid)

[3] The dates 1748, 1750, 1753, 1758 to 1762 indicate features listed in the registers of those years. The changes listed in the 1750 and 1759-1762 registers were almost certainly introduced the previous year.

double vertical pockets, each with six buttons set in pairs. From 1736: grey-white waistcoat, white gaiters. 1753: red waistcoat. 1758: grey-white coat, cuffs (four buttons), lining and breeches, red waistcoat, brass buttons, gold hat lace, double vertical pockets, each with six buttons set in pairs.

Navarre: Grey-white coat, cuffs (four buttons), lining, breeches and stockings, red waistcoat, brass buttons, gold hat lace, horizontal pocket with four buttons at each side and one at the bottom point. 1735: red breeches (Gudenus). From 1736: grey-white waistcoat, white gaiters. 1753: red waistcoat. 1758: grey-white coat, cuffs (five buttons), lining and breeches, red waistcoat, brass buttons, gold hat lace, horizontal pocket with four buttons at each side and one at the bottom point.

Piédmont: Grey-white coat, lining, breeches and stockings, grey-white cuffs changed to black around 1730, red waistcoat, brass buttons, gold hat lace, horizontal pocket with one button at each side and three at the bottom. Officers and NCOs had black velvet cuffs. 1735: grey-white waistcoat (Gudenus). From 1736: grey-white waistcoat, white gaiters. The officers seem to have kept their red waistcoats until 1751, as it was then decided they would have them the same colour (grey-white) as their men. 1758: grey-white coat, lining, waistcoat, breeches and stockings, black cuffs, brass buttons, gold hat lace, horizontal pocket with two buttons at each side and one at the bottom.

Normandie: Grey-white coat, cuffs and lining, red waistcoat, breeches and stockings, pewter buttons, white buttonhole and edging lace on waistcoat, silver hat lace. 1736: grey-white waistcoat and stockings and white gaiters. 1738: black velvet cuffs for officers. 1753: black cuffs for all. 1758: grey-white coat, lining, waistcoat and breeches, black cuffs and collar, pewter buttons, silver hat lace, black lapels on the waistcoat.

La Marine: Grey-white coat, cuffs, lining, breeches and stockings, red waistcoat, brass buttons, gold hat lace. Officers and NCOs had black velvet cuffs. 1735: grey-white waistcoat with two rows of buttons (Gudenus). From 1736: grey-white waistcoat, white gaiters. 1758: grey-white coat, lining and breeches, black collar and cuffs, red waistcoat, brass buttons, gold hat lace. 1760: orange buttonhole lace, gold for officers.

Colour bearers, Bourbon Regiment, c.1720. Left: the all-white colonel's colour; right: the regimental colour – white cross, blue upper left quarter, red upper right, black lower left, brown lower right. (Print after Delaistre)

Fusilier, Lyonnois Regiment, c.1720. This was the typical appearance of soldiers in the early part of the reign. (Print after Delaistre)

Bourbonnois: Grey-white coat, cuffs, lining, breeches and stockings, red waistcoat, brass buttons, gold hat lace, double vertical pockets, each with six buttons set in pairs. From 1736: grey-white waistcoat, white gaiters, four buttons on cuffs. 1753: red waistcoat. 1758: grey-white coat, cuffs (four buttons), lining, waistcoat and breeches, brass buttons, gold hat lace, double vertical pockets, each with six buttons set in pairs.

Leuville, 1718 Richelieu, 1738 Rohan-Chabot, 1745 Crillon, 1746 La Tour-du-Pin, 1761 Boisgelin, 1762 Béarn: Grey-white coat, cuffs, lining, breeches and stockings, grey-white collar edged red, red waistcoat, brass buttons, white buttonhole lace on waistcoat, gold hat lace. 1735: red coat lining, no lace on waistcoat (Gudenus). From 1736: grey-white waistcoat, white gaiters. 1753: red collar and waistcoat. 1758: grey-white coat, cuffs, lining, waistcoat and breeches, grey-white collar edged red, brass buttons, gold hat lace.

Auvergne: Grey-white coat, cuffs, lining, breeches and stockings, violet waistcoat, pewter buttons, white buttonhole lace on waistcoat, silver hat lace. From 1736: grey-white waistcoat, white gaiters. 1753: violet cuffs and collar. 1758: grey-white coat, lining, waistcoat and breeches, violet cuffs and collar, pewter buttons, silver hat lace.

Tallard, 1739 Monaco, 1749 Belzunce, 1761 Rougé, 1762 Flandres: Grey-white coat, cuffs, lining, waistcoat, breeches and stockings, brass buttons, yellow buttonhole lace on waistcoat, gold hat lace. From 1736: grey-white waistcoat, white gaiters. 1748: violet velvet cuffs for officers. 1753: violet cuffs and collar for all. 1758: grey-white coat, lining, waistcoat and breeches, violet cuffs and collar, brass buttons, gold hat lace.

Boufflers-Rémiancourt, 1718 Pons, 1735 Marsan, 1743 Bouzols, 1745 Mailly, 1758 Talaru, 1761 Chastellux, 1762 Guyenne: Grey-white coat, cuffs, lining, breeches and stockings, green waistcoat, pewter buttons, orange buttonhole lace and edging on waistcoat, gold hat lace, vertical pocket. 1735: no lace on waistcoat (Gudenus). From 1736: grey-white waistcoat, brass buttons, gold hat lace, white gaiters. 1753: red waistcoat. 1758: grey-white coat, collar, cuffs, lining and breeches, red waistcoat, brass buttons, gold hat lace, vertical pocket.

Du Roi: Grey-white coat, blue cuffs, lining, waistcoat, breeches and stockings, brass buttons set in threes, orange pointed buttonhole lace, gold hat lace. Sergeants had gold lace instead of orange for buttonholes. From 1736: white gaiters. 1753: blue collar. 1758 and 1763: same as above. Drummers: king's livery. According to Delaistre and a c.1718-37 clothing bill, the drummers of Du Roi had coats laced with the 'grand' livery lace and had an orange cross with a gold *fleur de lis* at the ends, which was worn on the chest and the back, as would befit the king's own regiment. The waistcoat and breeches were the same as the men's.

Royal: Grey-white coat, blue cuffs, lining, waistcoat and breeches, red stockings, pewter buttons, white buttonhole lace and edging on the waistcoat, silver hat lace, double vertical pockets, each with two buttons at the top and bottom and one at the centre. From 1736: blue collar, vertical pockets, each with five buttons set evenly, white gaiters. 1748: blue collar, waistcoat and breeches, gold hat lace. 1753: double vertical pockets with three buttons each, white breeches. 1758: grey-white coat, lining and breeches, blue cuffs, collar and waistcoat, pewter buttons, silver hat lace, double vertical pockets.

Poitou: Grey-white coat, blue cuffs (four buttons), lining, waistcoat, breeches and stockings, brass buttons, yellow buttonhole lace on the waistcoat, gold hat lace, double vertical pockets, each with six buttons set in pairs. From 1736: grey-white waistcoat and breeches, white gaiters. 1753: blue collar and waistcoat. 1758: grey-white coat, lining and breeches, blue cuffs (four buttons in pairs), collar and waistcoat, brass buttons, gold hat lace, double vertical pockets, each with six buttons set in pairs.

Lyonnois: Grey-white coat, red cuffs, lining and stockings, green waistcoat, grey-white breeches, brass buttons, gold hat lace, double vertical pockets. 1735: red breeches (Gudenus). From 1736: grey-white lining and waistcoat, white gaiters. 1753: red collar and waistcoat. 1758: grey-white coat, lining and breeches, red cuffs, collar and waistcoat, brass buttons, gold hat lace, double vertical pockets, each with three buttons. Drummers wore livery of Villeroi family until 1734, then king's livery, with red waistcoat and breeches according to a 1745 clothing bill.

Dauphin: Grey-white coat, blue cuffs (nine buttons), lining, waistcoat, breeches and stockings, brass buttons, orange buttonhole lace and edging on the waistcoat, gold hat lace, double vertical pockets, each with nine buttons set in threes. From 1736: grey-white lining, waistcoat and breeches, white gaiters. 1753: blue collar, lining and waistcoat. 1758: grey-white coat, lining and breeches, blue cuffs (nine buttons), collar and waistcoat, brass buttons, gold hat lace, double vertical pockets, each with nine buttons set in threes.

La Gervesais, 1734 D'Antin, 1743 Grondin, 1745 Montboissier, 1751 Joyeuse, 1755 Vaubecourt, 1762 Aunis: Grey-white coat, cuffs (four buttons), lining and breeches, red waistcoat and stockings, pewter buttons, orange buttonhole lace and edging on the waistcoat, silver hat lace. From 1736: five buttons on cuff, grey-white waistcoat, white gaiters. 1753: red waistcoat with white buttonhole lace. 1758: grey-white coat, cuffs (five buttons), lining and breeches, red collar and waistcoat, pewter buttons, silver hat lace, horizontal pocket with six buttons. 1760: red lapels, white buttonholes on lapels, grey-white waistcoat, pewter buttons, silver hat lace, horizontal pocket with five buttons.

Officer, Artois Regiment, c.1730. Grey-white coat, red waistcoat, gold buttons and lace. (Portrait at Fortress Louisbourg National Historic Site, Louisbourg, Canada)

Touraine: Grey-white coat, blue cuffs (five buttons), lining, waistcoat, breeches and stockings, brass buttons, orange buttonhole lace and edging on the waistcoat, gold hat lace, double vertical pockets, each with six buttons set in pairs. 1735: two rows of buttons and no lace on waistcoat (Gudenus). From 1736: grey-white lining, waistcoat and breeches, white gaiters, double vertical pockets, each with six buttons set evenly. From 1739: pewter buttons and silver hat lace. 1753: blue collar and waistcoat. 1758: grey-white coat, lining and breeches, blue cuffs (five buttons), collar and waistcoat, pewter buttons, silver hat lace, double vertical pockets, each with six buttons.

Anjou, 1753 Aquitaine: Grey-white coat, blue cuffs (four buttons), lining, waistcoat, breeches and stockings, brass buttons, gold hat lace, horizontal pocket with five buttons. From 1736: grey-white lining, waistcoat and breeches, white gaiters. 1753: blue collar, lining and waistcoat. 1758: grey-white coat, lining and breeches, blue cuffs (four buttons), collar and waistcoat, brass buttons, gold hat lace, horizontal pocket with five buttons.

Maine, 1736 Eu *or* **D'Eu:** Grey-white coat, blue cuffs, lining, waistcoat, breeches and stockings, brass buttons, orange buttonhole lace set in pairs on the waistcoat, gold hat lace, double vertical pockets, each with nine buttons set in threes. From 1736: grey-white lining, waistcoat and breeches, white gaiters, 'ordinary' cuffs and horizontal pockets with three buttons. 1753: blue waistcoat. 1758: grey-white coat, lining and breeches, blue cuffs, collar and waistcoat, brass buttons, gold hat lace.

Saillant, 1732 Estaing, 1734 Noailles, 1744 Custines, 1749 Saint-Chaumond, 1762 Dauphiné: Grey-white coat, blue cuffs, lining, waistcoat and breeches, red stockings, brass buttons, orange buttonhole lace on the waistcoat, gold hat lace, horizontal pocket with three buttons on each side and one at bottom point. From 1736: grey-white lining, waistcoat and breeches, white gaiters. 1753: red collar and cuffs; officers had crimson collar and cuffs. 1758: grey-white coat, lining, waistcoat and breeches, red cuffs and collar, brass buttons, gold hat lace, horizontal pocket with three buttons on each side and one at bottom point. 1760: crimson collar, cuffs and lapels.

Tourville, 1734 Meuse, 1738 Montmorin, 1762 Ile-de-France: Grey-white coat, lining and breeches, red cuffs and stockings, yellow waistcoat, brass buttons, gold hat lace, double vertical pockets, each with six buttons set in pairs. From 1736: grey-white waistcoat and breeches, white gaiters. 1753: red collar and waistcoat. 1758: grey-white coat, lining and breeches, red cuffs, collar and waistcoat, brass buttons, gold hat lace, double vertical pockets, each with six buttons set in pairs.

La Chesnelaye, 1730 Souvré, 1743 Lauraguais, 1745 Ségur, 1749 Briqueville, 1762 Soissonnois: Grey-white coat and breeches, red cuffs, lining, waistcoat and stockings, brass buttons, gold hat

Soldier of the Touraine Regiment, 1735, by Gudenus. Hat laced with false silver, white cockade, black cravat tied in a bow, grey-white coat, blue collar, cuffs, lining, waistcoat (lined with off-white) and breeches, pewter buttons and white gaiters. The collar was a new style but the coat still had buttons all the way down the front. (Private collection. Photo courtesy A.U. Koch)

lace. From 1736: grey-white lining and waistcoat, white gaiters. 1753: red waistcoat for officers. 1758: grey-white coat, lining, waistcoat and breeches, red cuffs and collar, brass buttons, gold hat lace.

La Reine: Grey-white coat and lining, red cuffs (five buttons) and stockings, blue waistcoat and breeches, pewter buttons, white buttonhole lace on the waistcoat, silver hat lace, horizontal pocket with four buttons on each side and one at bottom point. From 1736: grey-white waistcoat and breeches, white gaiters. 1753: blue waistcoat. 1758: grey-white coat, lining and breeches, red cuffs and collar, blue waistcoat, pewter buttons, silver hat lace, horizontal pocket with four buttons on each side.

Limousin: Grey-white coat, red cuffs (four buttons), lining, waistcoat, breeches and stockings, brass buttons, gold hat lace, horizontal pocket with four buttons. From 1736: grey-white lining, waistcoat and breeches, white gaiters. 1753: red collar and waistcoat. 1758: grey-white coat, lining and breeches, red cuffs (four buttons), collar and waistcoat, brass buttons, gold hat lace, horizontal pocket with four buttons.

Royal-Vaisseaux: Grey-white coat, blue cuffs (six buttons) and lining, red waistcoat, breeches and stockings, brass buttons, gold hat lace, double vertical pockets. Gudenus shows three buttons on cuff in 1735. From 1736: grey-white lining and breeches, red waistcoat, white gaiters. 1753: blue collar. 1758: grey-white coat, lining and breeches, blue cuffs (six buttons) and collar, red waistcoat, brass buttons, gold hat lace, double vertical pockets, each with three buttons.

Orléans: Grey-white coat, lining and breeches, red cuffs (four buttons), waistcoat and stockings, brass buttons, gold hat lace, horizontal pocket with four buttons. From 1736: grey-white waistcoat, white gaiters. 1753: red waistcoat. 1758: grey-white coat, lining and breeches, red cuffs (four buttons), collar and waistcoat, brass buttons, gold hat lace, horizontal pocket with four buttons.

La Couronne: Grey-white coat, blue cuffs, lining, waistcoat, breeches and stockings, pewter buttons, silver hat lace. 1735: red and black flat aiguillette (Gudenus). From 1736: grey-white lining, waistcoat and breeches, white gaiters, gold hat lace. 1753: blue collar and waistcoat. Red and black aiguillettes for sergeants and grenadiers. 1758: grey-white coat, lining and breeches, blue cuffs, collar and waistcoat, pewter buttons, silver hat lace.

Bretagne: Grey-white coat, cuffs (four buttons) and lining, red waistcoat, breeches and stockings, brass buttons, yellow buttonhole lace and edging on the waistcoat, gold hat lace, horizontal pocket with four buttons. 1735: red cuffs, two rows of buttons and no lace on waistcoat (Gudenus). From 1736: grey-white cuffs, waistcoat and breeches, white gaiters, vertical pocket. 1753: grey-white collar and red waistcoat. 1758: grey-white coat, cuffs (four buttons), lining and breeches, black collar, red waistcoat, pewter buttons, silver hat lace, horizontal pocket with

Soldier of the Saintonge regiment with his girlfriend, 1735, by Gudenus. Hat laced with false gold, white cockade, black cravat tied in a bow, grey-white coat and breeches, blue collar, cuffs, lining and waistcoat, brass buttons and white gaiters. The coat is cut in the latest style, with a collar and with buttons going down to just below the waist – a feature made official in 1736. The girl has a red skirt, a white and beige apron and bodice, a white blouse, a 'mug' cap and a straw hat. (Private collection. Photo courtesy A.U. Koch)

four buttons. 1762: blue coat, cuffs, lining, waistcoat and breeches, white aiguillette, pewter buttons, white buttonhole lace, silver hat lace.

Perche, 1744 amalgamated with Gardes Lorraines: Grey-white coat, red cuffs, lining, waistcoat, breeches and stockings, pewter buttons, silver hat lace, double vertical pockets. From 1736: grey-white lining, waistcoat and breeches, white gaiters, vertical pocket.

Artois: Grey-white coat, cuffs (six buttons), lining and breeches, red waistcoat and stockings, brass buttons, yellow buttonhole lace on the waistcoat, gold hat lace, horizontal pocket with three buttons at each side and three below. From 1736: grey-white waistcoat, white gaiters. 1753: red waistcoat. 1758: grey-white coat, cuffs (six buttons), lining and breeches, red waistcoat, brass buttons, gold hat lace, horizontal pocket with three buttons at each side and three below. 1760: red breeches.

Louvigny, 1734 Rochechouart, 1743 Aubeterre, 1745 Rohan, 1759 Montrevel, 1762 Berry: Grey-white coat and lining, red cuffs, waistcoat, breeches and stockings, pewter buttons, white buttonhole lace and edging on the waistcoat, silver hat lace. From 1736: grey-white waistcoat and breeches, white gaiters. 1753: red waistcoat. 1758: grey-white coat, lining and breeches, red cuffs, collar and waistcoat, pewter buttons, silver hat lace.

Barrois, 1716 Vendôme, 1726 Ouroy, 1743 Stinville, 1745 La Roche-Aymon, 1761 Montmorency (also called Royan), 1762 Hainault: Grey-white coat, cuffs, lining and breeches, red waistcoat and stockings, pewter buttons, silver hat lace. From 1736: grey-white waistcoat, brass buttons, white gaiters. From c.1743: red cuffs, pewter buttons. 1753: two buttons only on cuff, red waistcoat, brass buttons. 1758: grey-white coat, lining and breeches, red cuffs, collar and waistcoat, brass buttons, gold hat lace.

La Sarre: Grey-white coat and breeches, blue cuffs and lining, red waistcoat and stockings, brass buttons, gold hat lace. From 1736: grey-white lining, waistcoat and breeches, white gaiters. 1753: blue collar, red waistcoat. 1758: grey-white coat, lining and breeches, blue cuffs and collar, red waistcoat, brass buttons, gold hat lace.

La Fère: Grey-white coat, lining, breeches and stockings, red cuffs and waistcoat, pewter buttons, gold hat lace. 1735: red breeches, white hat lace (Gudenus). From 1736: grey-white waistcoat, white gaiters. 1753: red collar and waistcoat. 1758: grey-white coat, lining, waistcoat and breeches, red cuffs and collar, pewter buttons, gold hat lace. 1762: red lapels.

Royal-Roussillon: Grey-white coat, blue cuffs (six buttons), lining, waistcoat, breeches and stockings, brass buttons, orange buttonhole lace on the waistcoat, gold hat lace. From 1736: grey-white lining, waistcoat and breeches, white gaiters. 1753: blue collar, lining, waistcoat and breeches. c.1755: grey-white lining and breeches. 1758: grey-white coat, lining and breeches, blue cuffs (six buttons), collar and waistcoat, brass buttons, gold hat lace.

Fusilier, Du Roi Regiment, c.1750. The cockade is shown as blue and white, apparently a regimental peculiarity. The men working in the background wear shirts, blue waistcoat and breeches and forage caps of blue with white turnups decorated with three yellow *fleurs de lis*. (Print after contemporary painting)

Condé: Grey-white coat, lining and breeches, red cuffs (five buttons), waistcoat and stockings, brass buttons, gold hat lace, horizontal pocket with five buttons. From 1736: grey-white waistcoat, white gaiters. 1753: red waistcoat. 1758: grey-white coat, lining and breeches, red cuffs (five buttons), collar and waistcoat, brass buttons, gold hat lace, horizontal pocket with five buttons.

Bourbon: Grey-white coat, red cuffs (six buttons), lining, waistcoat, breeches and stockings, pewter buttons, silver hat lace, double vertical pockets, each with six buttons. From 1736: grey-white lining, waistcoat and breeches, white gaiters, double vertical pockets, each with six buttons set in threes. 1753: red collar and waistcoat. 1758: grey-white coat, lining and breeches, red cuffs (five buttons), collar and waistcoat, pewter buttons, silver hat lace, double vertical pockets, each with six buttons set in threes.

Beauvoisis: Grey-white coat, cuffs, lining and breeches, red waistcoat and stockings, pewter buttons, silver hat lace, double vertical pockets, each with six buttons set in pairs. 1735: red breeches (Gudenus). From 1736: grey-white waistcoat and breeches, white gaiters, double vertical pockets, each with six buttons set evenly. 1753: grey-white collar, red waistcoat. 1758: grey-white coat, collar, cuffs, lining and breeches, red waistcoat, pewter buttons, silver hat lace, double vertical pockets, each with six buttons.

Rouergue: Grey-white coat and lining, red cuffs, waistcoat, breeches and stockings, brass buttons, orange buttonhole lace and edging on the waistcoat, gold hat lace. From 1736: grey-white waistcoat and breeches, white gaiters, red collar. 1753: red waistcoat. 1758: grey-white coat, lining and breeches, red cuffs, collar and waistcoat, brass buttons, gold hat lace.

Bourgogne: Grey-white coat, cuffs and lining, red waistcoat, breeches and stockings, brass buttons, gold hat lace. From 1736: grey-white

The Royal-Comtois Regiment marching towards Antibes in 1755. The men are loaded up with haversacks, muskets and essentials such as tent poles. The drummer carries his drum on his back. A sick or exhausted soldier is on a baggage wagon with women and a child. (Detail of a copy of a painting by Joseph Vernet, Musée Naval et Napoléonien, Cap d'Antibes)

waistcoat and breeches, white gaiters. 1753: red waistcoat. 1758: grey-white coat, collar, cuffs, lining and breeches, red waistcoat, brass buttons, gold hat lace.

Royal-Marine: Grey-white coat, blue cuffs, lining, waistcoat and breeches, red stockings, pewter buttons, silver hat lace. 1735: blue collar (Gudenus). From 1736: grey-white lining, waistcoat and breeches, white gaiters. 1753: blue waistcoat, blue velvet cuffs for officers. 1758: grey-white coat, lining and breeches, blue cuffs, collar and waistcoat, pewter buttons, silver hat lace.

Vermandois: Grey-white coat, red cuffs, lining, breeches and stockings, blue waistcoat and stockings, brass buttons, gold hat lace, double vertical pockets, each with six buttons set in pairs. From 1736: grey-white lining, waistcoat and breeches, white gaiters. 1753: red collar and pocket edging, blue waistcoat. 1758: grey-white coat, lining and breeches, red cuffs and collar, blue waistcoat, brass buttons, gold hat lace, double vertical pockets, each with six buttons set in pairs. 1760: pockets piped red.

Languedoc: Grey-white coat, blue cuffs, lining, waistcoat and breeches, red stockings, brass buttons, orange lace edging waistcoat, gold hat lace, horizontal pocket with three buttons on each side. From 1736: grey-white lining, waistcoat and waistcoat. 1753: blue collar, lining and waistcoat. 1758: grey-white coat, lining and breeches, blue cuffs, collar and waistcoat, brass buttons, gold hat lace, horizontal pocket with three buttons on each side. 1761: blue lapels, grey-white waistcoat, blue piping edging coat and waistcoat.

Infantry tools and equipment. At the centre (A) is the 'ordinary' or common rough linen or sailcloth haversack with its small cow hide bag. The haversack is carried by a leather belt with a brass buckle. Below (B) is a haversack with double straps, a bag-like knapsack, with its small cow hide bag at lower left. The other figures show the carrying case, usually of leather with narrow leather straps, for various types of tools. Below right is a typical small shovel carried by soldiers. (Engraving in La Poterie's *Institutions Militaires*... 1754)

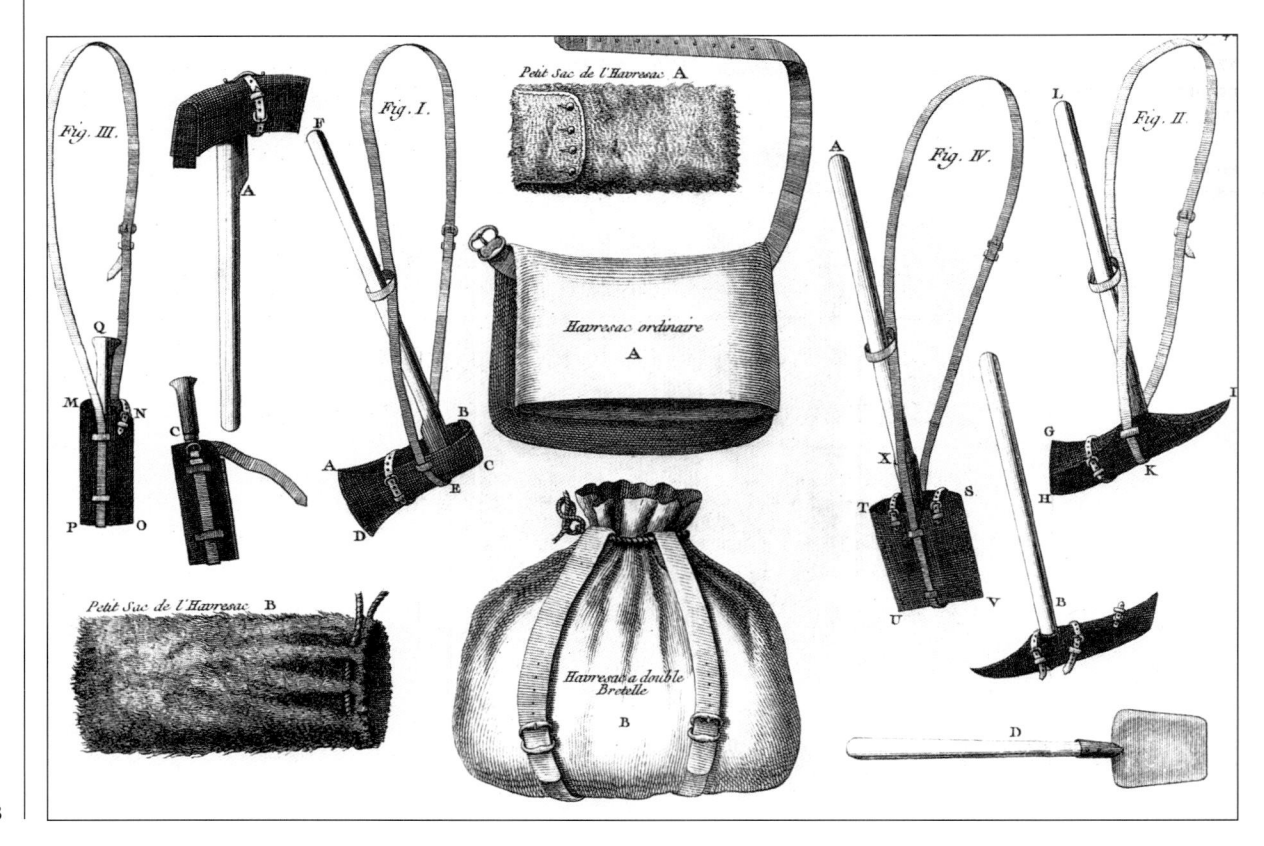

Sourches, 1718 Saint-Simon, 1734 Puyguyon, 1742 Revel, 1745 Talaru, 1758 Aumont, 1762 Beauce: Grey-white coat, cuffs and lining, red waistcoat, breeches and stockings, brass buttons, white buttonhole lace and edging on waistcoat, gold hat lace. From 1736: grey-white waistcoat and breeches, white gaiters; five buttons to horizontal pocket later on. 1753: grey-white collar, bearskin caps for grenadiers. 1758: grey-white coat, collar, cuffs (five buttons), lining and breeches, red waistcoat, brass buttons, gold hat lace, horizontal pocket with five buttons.

Médoc: Grey-white coat, lining and breeches, red cuffs, waistcoat and stockings, pewter buttons, silver hat lace. From 1736: grey-white waistcoat, white gaiters. 1753: red collar and waistcoat. 1758: grey-white coat, lining and breeches, red cuffs, collar and waistcoat, pewter buttons, silver hat lace.

Gensac, 1734 Duras, 1743 Bonnac, 1749 Cossé-Brissac *or* Brissac, 1759 Lemps, 1761 Puységur, 1762 Viverais: Grey-white coat and lining, red cuffs (five buttons), waistcoat, breeches and stockings, brass buttons, orange buttonhole lace and edging on waistcoat, gold hat lace, horizontal pocket with five buttons. From 1736: grey-white waistcoat and breeches, white gaiters. 1753: red waistcoat, 'ordinary' pockets and cuffs. 1758: grey-white coat, lining and breeches, red cuffs (five buttons), collar and waistcoat, brass buttons, gold hat lace, horizontal pockets with five buttons.

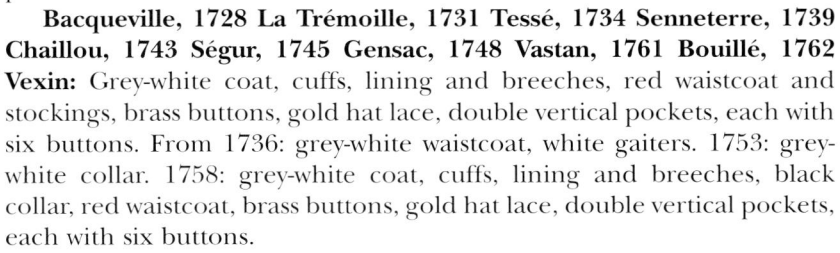

Bacqueville, 1728 La Trémoille, 1731 Tessé, 1734 Senneterre, 1739 Chaillou, 1743 Ségur, 1745 Gensac, 1748 Vastan, 1761 Bouillé, 1762 Vexin: Grey-white coat, cuffs, lining and breeches, red waistcoat and stockings, brass buttons, gold hat lace, double vertical pockets, each with six buttons. From 1736: grey-white waistcoat, white gaiters. 1753: grey-white collar. 1758: grey-white coat, cuffs, lining and breeches, black collar, red waistcoat, brass buttons, gold hat lace, double vertical pockets, each with six buttons.

Royal-Comtois: Grey-white coat, blue cuffs, lining, waistcoat and breeches, brass buttons, orange buttonhole lace and edging on waistcoat, gold hat lace, double vertical pockets, each with nine buttons set in threes. From 1736: grey-white lining, waistcoat and breeches, white gaiters. 1753: blue collar and waistcoat; officers had buttons on both sides on the coat's front. 1758: grey-white coat, lining and breeches, blue cuffs, collar and waistcoat, brass buttons, gold hat lace, double vertical pockets, each with six buttons set in threes.

Lyonne, 1723 Montconseil, 1742 Traisnel, 1757 Brancas, 1758 Durfort, 1761 Lastic, 1762 Beaujolais: Grey-white coat, cuffs (five buttons), lining and breeches, red waistcoat and stockings, brass buttons, orange buttonhole lace on waistcoat, gold hat lace, horizontal pocket with two buttons on each side and one below at the point. From 1736: grey-white waistcoat, white gaiters. 1758: uniform completely grey-white, brass buttons, gold hat lace, five buttons on cuffs, horizontal pocket with two buttons on each side and one below at the point. 1762: crimson collar and lapels.

Grenadier officer's cartridge box, 1758-1767. This cartridge box is according to the order of 9 December 1758. Its reddish-brown leather flap has a gold embroidered grenade and gold edging. (Musée du Royal 22ᵉ Régiment, Quebec City)

BELOW **Front view, drum case of the Royal-Roussillon Regiment, 1756. Regimental drum cases were painted with the coat of arms in front, flanked by regimental colours. Cannons were very often painted below, but only for decoration; they had no affiliation to artillery units. Hoops could be blue, red, or red and white. (Musée de l'Armée, Château de l'Empéri, Salon-de-Provence)**

BELOW, RIGHT **Back view, drum case of the Royal-Roussillon Regiment, 1756. This fine example has the blue case strewn with large lilies. It carries the name of the regiment and that of the company, La Barière's company of the 1st Battalion. It was made in January 1756 by Germain Allier, whose shop was at the Place de la Belle Croix in Nîmes. (Musée de l'Armée, Château de l'Empéri, Salon-de-Provence)**

Provence: Grey-white coat, lining and breeches, red cuffs (nine buttons), waistcoat and stockings, brass buttons, orange lace edging the waistcoat, silver hat lace, horizontal pocket with four buttons. 1735: no lace on waistcoat (Gudenus). From 1736: grey-white waistcoat, white gaiters. 1753: red collar and waistcoat. 1758: grey-white coat, lining and breeches, red cuffs (eight buttons), collar and waistcoat, brass buttons, gold hat lace, horizontal pockets with five buttons; sergeants had silver lace edging their cuffs and silver hat lace.

Laval, 1729 Tonnay-Charente, 1731 Mortemart, 1749 Cambis, December 1762 incorporated into Royal: Grey-white coat, lining and breeches, red cuffs, waistcoat and stockings, alternating brass and pewter buttons, gold and silver hat lace. From 1736: grey-white waistcoat, white gaiters. 1753: red collar and waistcoat. 1758: grey-white coat, lining and breeches, red cuffs, collar and waistcoat, brass and pewter buttons, gold and silver hat lace.

Ilsenghein, 1717 Mailly, 1735 Biron, 1745 Rohan-Rochefort, 1761 Saint-Mauris, 1762 Poitou: Grey-white coat and breeches, red cuffs, lining, waistcoat and stockings, brass buttons, gold hat lace. From 1736: grey-white lining, waistcoat, white gaiters. 1753: red collar and waistcoat, yellow buttonholes on the cuffs and waistcoat. 1758: grey-white coat, lining, waistcoat and breeches, red cuffs and collar, brass buttons, gold hat lace, red lapels on waistcoat.

Nice, December 1762 incorporated into Lyonnois: Grey-white coat and cuffs, red lining, waistcoat, breeches and stockings, brass buttons, white buttonhole lace on the waistcoat, gold hat lace, vertical pocket. 1735: no lace on waistcoat (Gudenus). From 1736: grey-white lining, waistcoat and breeches, white gaiters. 1753: red waistcoat. 1758: grey-white coat, collar, cuffs lining and breeches, red waistcoat, brass buttons, gold hat lace, vertical pockets.

Toulouse, 1734 Penthièvre: Grey-white coat, blue cuffs, lining, waistcoat, breeches and stockings, brass buttons, white buttonhole lace on the waistcoat, silver hat lace. From 1736: grey-white lining, waistcoat and breeches, white gaiters, pewter buttons. 1753: blue collar and waistcoat. 1758: grey-white coat, lining and breeches, blue cuffs, collar and waistcoat, pewter buttons, silver hat lace.

Guyenne, December 1762 incorporated into Dauphin: Grey-white coat, lining and breeches, red cuffs, waistcoat and stockings, brass buttons, gold hat lace. From 1736: grey-white waistcoat, white gaiters. 1753: red waistcoat. 1758: grey-white coat, lining and breeches, red cuffs, collar and waistcoat, brass buttons, gold hat lace.

Lorraine, December 1762 incorporated into Aunis: Grey-white coat, cuffs, lining and breeches, red waistcoat and stockings, brass buttons, gold hat lace. From 1736: grey-white waistcoat, white gaiters. 1753: red waistcoat. 1758: grey-white coat, collar, cuffs, lining and breeches, red waistcoat, brass buttons, gold hat lace.

Flandres, December 1762 incorporated into Touraine: Grey-white coat, blue cuffs (four buttons), lining, waistcoat and breeches, red stockings, brass and pewter buttons, gold hat lace, horizontal pocket with four buttons at bottom and one above to each side. From 1736: grey-white lining, waistcoat and breeches, white gaiters. 1753: blue collar and waistcoat, silver and gold hat lace. 1758: grey-white coat, lining and breeches, blue cuffs (four buttons), collar and waistcoat, brass and pewter buttons, gold and silver hat lace, horizontal pocket with two buttons at bottom and two to each side.

Berry, December 1762 incorporated into Aquitaine: Grey-white coat and lining, red cuffs (five buttons), waistcoat, breeches and stockings, brass buttons, gold hat lace, double vertical pockets. From 1736: grey-white waistcoat and breeches, white gaiters. 1753: red collar and waistcoat. 1758: grey-white coat, lining and breeches, red collar, cuffs (five buttons) and waistcoat, brass buttons, gold hat lace, double vertical pockets.

Béarn, raised 1684; disbanded December 1762: Grey-white coat, lining and breeches, red cuffs, waistcoat and stockings, brass buttons, gold hat lace, double vertical pockets. From 1736: grey-white waistcoat and breeches, white gaiters. 1753: red waistcoat. 1758: grey-white coat, lining and breeches, red collar, cuffs and waistcoat, brass buttons, gold hat lace, double vertical pockets.

Haynault *or* Hainaut, disbanded December 1762: Grey-white coat, lining and breeches, red cuffs, waistcoat and stockings, brass buttons, gold hat lace, horizontal pocket with three buttons to each side and one at the bottom point. From 1736: grey-white waistcoat, white gaiters. 1753: red collar and waistcoat, bearskin cap for grenadiers. 1758: grey-white coat, lining and breeches, red collar, cuffs and waistcoat, brass buttons, gold hat lace, horizontal pocket with nine buttons.

Boulonnois: Grey-white coat and breeches, blue cuffs, lining, waistcoat and stockings, brass buttons, silver hat lace, round pocket with eight buttons. From 1736: grey-white lining, kept the blue waistcoat and breeches, white gaiters, horizontal pocket with three buttons to each side. 1753: blue collar. 1758: grey-white coat, lining and breeches, blue collar, cuffs (four buttons) and waistcoat, brass buttons, gold hat lace, shield-shaped pocket with eight buttons.

Angoumois: Grey-white coat and lining, blue cuffs, red waistcoat and breeches, brass buttons, gold hat lace. From 1736: grey-white waistcoat and breeches, white gaiters. 1753: blue collar and waistcoat, pewter

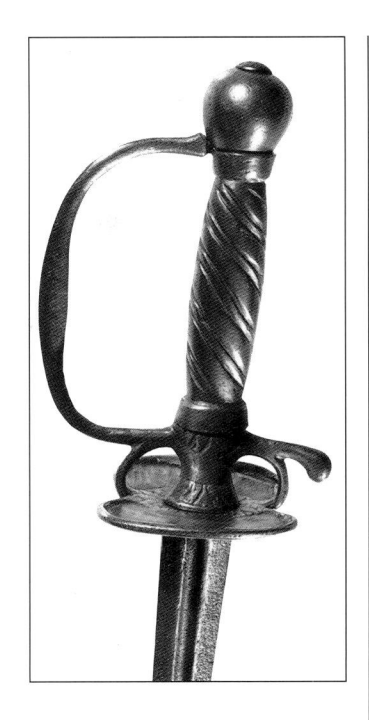

Fusilier private's sword hilt, c.1680s–1764. Common soldiers were issued cheap, straight-bladed swords with brass hilts, often with a cast brass grip, as shown here. This Mousquetaire-style hilt was very common until about 1750, when a half shell type also became popular. (Fortress Louisbourg National Historic Site)

buttons, silver hat lace. 1758: grey-white coat, cuffs, lining and breeches, red collar, blue waistcoat, pewter buttons, silver hat lace. 1760: blue collar.

Périgord: Grey-white coat and lining, blue cuffs, red waistcoat, breeches and stockings, brass buttons, gold hat lace. From 1736: grey-white waistcoat and breeches, white gaiters. 1753: blue collar, red waistcoat. 1758: grey-white coat, lining and breeches, blue cuffs, red collar and waistcoat, pewter buttons, silver hat lace.

Saintonge: Grey-white coat and stockings, blue cuffs, lining, waistcoat and breeches, white stockings, brass buttons, gold hat lace. From 1736: grey-white lining, waistcoat and breeches, white gaiters. 1753: blue waistcoat. 1758: grey-white coat, lining and breeches, blue collar, cuffs and waistcoat, brass buttons, gold hat lace.

Bigorre: Grey-white coat, lining, breeches and stockings, blue cuffs and waistcoat, brass buttons, gold hat lace. From 1736: grey-white waistcoat, white gaiters. 1753: blue waistcoat, velvet cuffs for officers. 1758: grey-white coat, lining and breeches, blue collar, cuffs and waistcoat, brass buttons, gold hat lace.

Forez, Forezt *or* Forest: Grey-white coat and lining, red cuffs, breeches and stockings, blue waistcoat, brass buttons, orange buttonhole lace on the waistcoat, gold hat lace. From 1736: grey-white waistcoat, white gaiters. 1753: red waistcoat. 1758: grey-white coat, lining and breeches, red collar, cuffs and waistcoat, brass buttons, gold hat lace.

Cambrésis: Grey-white coat, lining and breeches, red cuffs, waistcoat and stockings, brass buttons, yellow buttonhole lace and edging on the waistcoat, gold hat lace. From 1736: grey-white waistcoat, white gaiters, horizontal pocket with three buttons on each side and three at bottom. 1753: red waistcoat, officers had buttons on both sides of the coat's front. 1758: grey-white coat, lining and breeches, red collar, cuffs (six buttons) and waistcoat, brass buttons, gold hat lace, horizontal pocket with three buttons on each side and three at bottom.

Tournaisis: Grey-white coat, lining, breeches and stockings, red cuffs and waistcoat, brass buttons, gold hat lace, horizontal pocket with five buttons. From 1736: grey-white waistcoat, white gaiters. 1753: red waistcoat, six buttons on cuff. 1758: grey-white coat, lining and breeches, red collar, cuffs (five buttons) and waistcoat, brass buttons, gold hat lace, horizontal pocket with five buttons.

Foix: Grey-white coat and lining, red cuffs and stockings, blue waistcoat and breeches, brass buttons, silver hat lace. From 1736: red collar, grey-white waistcoat and breeches, white gaiters. 1753: light blue waistcoat, pocket flap edged red. 1758: grey-white coat, lining and breeches, red collar and cuffs, blue waistcoat, brass buttons, gold hat lace.

Bresse, disbanded November 1762: Grey-white coat and breeches, blue cuffs (six buttons), lining and waistcoat, red stockings, brass buttons, gold hat lace, horizontal pocket with five buttons. From 1736: grey-white collar, lining and waistcoat, white gaiters. 1753: blue collar and waistcoat, silver hat lace. 1758: grey-white coat, lining and breeches, blue collar, cuffs and waistcoat, brass buttons, gold hat lace, horizontal pocket with six buttons. 1760: blue breeches, yellow buttonhole lace, six buttons on cuff.

La Marche, disbanded November 1762: Grey-white coat, small standing collar, lining and breeches, red cuffs, waistcoat and stockings,

Sergeant's sword hilt, c.1756. Infantry sergeants had straight-bladed swords of better quality than the soldiers. This sergeant's model was introduced in 1756. It has a white metal guard with a black ebony grip. (Fortress Louisbourg National Historic Site)

Grenadier's sabre hilt, c.1750-1760. Grenadiers carried sturdy sabres, generally of good quality but of many types, since there were no set models. It usually had a brass hilt with a double-branched guard and a brass wire grip as shown. White metal guards were also popular. (David M. Stewart Museum, Montreal)

brass buttons, orange buttonhole lace and edging on the waistcoat, gold hat lace, horizontal pocket with five buttons. From 1736: grey-white collar and waistcoat, white gaiters. 1753: red waistcoat (collar not mentioned). 1758: grey-white coat, lining and breeches, red collar, cuffs and waistcoat, brass buttons, gold hat lace, horizontal pocket with five buttons.

Quercy: Grey-white coat, lining and breeches, red cuffs (four buttons), waistcoat and stockings, brass buttons, gold hat lace, horizontal pocket with five buttons. From 1736: grey-white waistcoat, white gaiters. 1750: silver hat lace. 1753: red collar and waistcoat, ordinary pockets. 1758: grey-white coat, lining and breeches, red collar, cuffs (five buttons) and waistcoat, brass buttons, gold hat lace, horizontal pocket with five buttons.

Nivernois, 1753 Comte de La Marche: Grey-white coat, lining and breeches, blue cuffs, red waistcoat and stockings, brass buttons, orange buttonhole lace on the waistcoat, gold hat lace, horizontal pocket with four buttons. From 1736: grey-white waistcoat, white gaiters, four buttons on cuffs. 1753: blue waistcoat. 1758: grey-white coat, lining and breeches, blue collar, cuffs (four buttons) and waistcoat, pewter buttons, silver hat lace, horizontal pocket with four buttons. Grenadier caps, presumably bearskins, reported captured by Prussian hussars in October 1758 (*Mémoires d'un militaire*, 1759). Drummers: king's livery to 1753, then colonel's livery.

Brie, disbanded November 1762: Grey-white coat, lining and breeches, red cuffs, waistcoat and stockings, brass buttons, gold hat lace, double vertical pockets, each with nine buttons set in threes. From 1736: grey-white waistcoat, white gaiters. 1753: red waistcoat. 1758: grey-white coat, lining and breeches, red collar, cuffs and waistcoat, brass buttons, gold hat lace, double vertical pockets, each with nine buttons set in threes.

Soissonnois, disbanded November 1762: Grey-white coat, blue cuffs (five buttons), lining, waistcoat, breeches and stockings, brass buttons, gold hat lace, horizontal pocket with five buttons. From 1736: grey-white lining, waistcoat and breeches, white gaiters. 1753: blue collar, lining and waistcoat, ordinary pockets. 1758: grey-white coat, lining and breeches, blue collar, cuffs (five buttons) and waistcoat, brass buttons, gold hat lace, horizontal pocket with five buttons.

Île-de-France, disbanded November 1762: Grey-white coat and lining, blue cuffs, lining, waistcoat, breeches and stockings, brass buttons, gold hat lace, double vertical pockets. From 1736: grey-white lining, waistcoat and breeches, white gaiters. 1753: blue waistcoat. 1758: grey-white coat, lining and breeches, blue collar, cuffs and waistcoat, brass buttons, gold hat lace, double vertical pockets.

Vexin, incorporated into Vermandois March 1749: Grey-white coat, blue cuffs (four buttons with white buttonholes), lining, waistcoat, breeches and stockings, brass buttons, orange buttonhole lace and edging on the waistcoat, gold hat lace, vertical pocket with four buttons. From 1736: grey-white lining, waistcoat and breeches, white gaiters, vertical pocket with four buttons one top and bottom, two in the middle.

Aunis, incorporated into Languedoc March 1749: Grey-white coat, lining and breeches, red cuffs, waistcoat and stockings, brass buttons, gold hat lace. From 1736: grey-white waistcoat, white gaiters.

Beauce, incorporated into Talaru March 1749: Grey-white coat, red cuffs, lining, waistcoat, breeches and stockings, brass buttons, yellow buttonhole lace and edging on the waistcoat, gold hat lace, double vertical pockets. From 1736: grey-white lining, waistcoat and breeches, white gaiters.

Dauphiné, incorporated into Médoc March 1749: Grey-white coat and lining, blue cuffs (five buttons), red waistcoat, breeches and stockings, brass buttons, silver hat lace, horizontal pocket with five buttons. From 1736: grey-white waistcoat and breeches, white gaiters.

Viverais, incorporated into Bonnac March 1749: Grey-white coat, lining and breeches, red cuffs, waistcoat and stockings, brass buttons, gold hat lace, horizontal pocket with two buttons to each side and one at the bottom point. From 1736: grey-white waistcoat, white gaiters.

Luxembourg, incorporated into Vastan March 1749: Grey-white coat, lining and breeches, blue cuffs, waistcoat and stockings, pewter buttons, white buttonhole lace on waistcoat, silver hat lace. From 1736: grey-white waistcoat, white gaiters. 1748: blue collar.

Bassigny, incorporated into Royal-Comtois March 1749: Grey-white coat, lining and breeches, blue cuffs, red waistcoat and stockings, brass buttons, gold hat lace. From 1736: grey-white waistcoat, white gaiters.

Beaujolois, incorporated into Traisnel March 1749: Grey-white coat and lining, red cuffs, waistcoat, breeches and stockings, brass buttons, gold hat lace, double vertical pockets. From 1736: grey-white waistcoat and breeches, white gaiters.

Ponthieu, incorporated into Provence March 1749: Grey-white coat, red cuffs, lining, waistcoat, breeches and stockings, pewter buttons, silver hat lace, white buttonhole lace and edging on waistcoat, double vertical pockets. From 1736: grey-white lining, waistcoat and breeches, white gaiters.

Beaufort, 1729 Boufflers, 1727 La Vallière, 1747 Escars, incorporated into Cambis March 1749: Grey-white coat, lining and breeches, red cuffs (six buttons) and stockings, green waistcoat, brass buttons, gold hat lace, horizontal pocket with six buttons. From 1736: grey-white waistcoat, white gaiters.

Tessé, 1716 Olonne, 1721 Montmorency or Ligny, 1740 Beauffremont, 1744 Fleury, incorporated into Rochefort March 1749: Grey-white coat, lining, breeches and stockings, red cuffs and waistcoat, brass buttons, gold hat lace. From 1736: grey-white waistcoat, white gaiters.

Brichambault, 1719 Montfort, 1721 Picquigny, 1733 Rosnvinien, 1743 Montboissier, 1746 La Tour d'Auvergne, incorporated into Nice March 1749: Grey-white coat, lining and breeches, red cuffs, waistcoat and stockings, pewter buttons, silver hat lace. 1735: red breeches (Gudenus). From 1736: grey-white waistcoat and breeches, white gaiters.

La Sarre Regiment, 1757. This depiction of a soldier, in combat with green and red-coated enemies, shows a rare back view. The '1757 Ms' from which this plate is taken was in the former Ministry of War Library and is now in the Musée de l'Armée in Paris.

Gardes-Francaises
(The French Guards), 1740s and 1750s
1: Officer, full dress, 1740s and 1750s
2: Officer, undress, 1740s and 1750s
3: Private, 1740s and 1750s
4: Drummer, 1740s and 1750s

Infantry, 1720s
1: Tourville Regiment, sergeant
2: Du Roi Regiment, private
3: Lyonnois Regiment, drummer
4: Dauphin Regiment, officers

Infantry, Polish Succession War, 1734-35
1: Bourbonnois Regiment, drummer
2: Bretagne Regiment, private of grenadiers
3: Richelieu Regiment, sergeant
4: Royal-Roussillon Regiment, officer with colour and private

Infantry, Austrian Succession War, 1740s
1: Touraine Regiment, grenadier
2: Ponthieu Regiment, sergeant
3: Penthièvre Regiment, sergeant
4: Penthièvre Regiment, officers with colour

Infantry, 1750s
1: La Reine Regiment, drummer
2: Grenadiers de France Regiment, sergeant
3: Cambis Regiment, sergeant
4: Auvergne Regiment, officer with colour

E

Infantry in Canada, 1755-57
1: La Reine Regiment, sergeant
2: Languedoc Regiment, private
3: Guyenne Regiment, officer with regimental colour
4: Béarn Regiment, corporal

Infantry in Louisiana, the West Indies and India, 1758-63
1: Lorraine Regiment, grenadier, India, 1758-61
2 & 3: Angoumois Regiment, private and drummers, Louisiana, 1760-63
4: Grenadiers Royaux, private, Martinique and Haiti, 1760-63
5: Saint-Domingue Piquets, corporal, Haiti, 1761-63

Infantry, later part of Seven Years War, 1760-63
1: Bresse Regiment, sergeant
2: Vaubecourt Regiment, officer
3: Saint-Chaumond Regiment, grenadier
4: La Marne Regimnet, private

Chartres, 1724 Étampes, 1737 Chartres: Grey-white coat, lining and breeches, red cuffs, waistcoat and stockings, brass buttons, gold hat lace, shield-shaped pocket with five buttons. From 1736: grey-white waistcoat, white gaiters. 1753: red collar and waistcoat. 1758: grey-white coat, lining and breeches, red collar, cuffs and waistcoat, brass buttons, gold hat lace, shield-shaped pocket with five buttons.

Blasois, incorporated into Guyenne March 1749: Grey-white coat, red cuffs, lining, waistcoat, breeches and stockings, pewter buttons, silver hat lace, double vertical pockets, each with six buttons set in pairs. From 1736: grey-white collar, lining, waistcoat and breeches, white gaiters.

Gâtinois, incorporated into Lorraine March 1749: Grey-white coat, lining, red cuffs, waistcoat, breeches and stockings, pewter buttons, silver hat lace. From 1736: grey-white waistcoat and breeches, white gaiters.

Conty *or* Conti: Grey-white coat and stockings, blue cuffs, lining, waistcoat and breeches, pewter buttons, silver hat lace. From 1736: grey-white lining, waistcoat and breeches, white gaiters. 1750: red cuffs. 1753: blue cuffs and waistcoat. 1758: grey-white coat, lining and breeches, blue collar, cuffs and waistcoat, pewter buttons, silver hat lace.

Auxerrois, incorporated into Flandres March 1749: Grey-white coat, lining and breeches, red cuffs, waistcoat and stockings, pewter buttons, white buttonhole and edging lace on waistcoat, silver hat lace. From 1736: grey-white waistcoat, white gaiters.

Agenois, incorporated into Berry March 1749: Grey-white coat, lining and breeches, red cuffs, waistcoat and stockings, pewter buttons, silver hat lace, horizontal pocket with two buttons on each side and one at the bottom point. 1735: two rows of buttons on waistcoat, with white lace between the rows (Gudenus). From 1736: grey-white waistcoat, white gaiters.

Santerre, incorporated into Béarn March 1749: Grey-white coat and breeches, blue cuffs and lining, red waistcoat and stockings, brass buttons, orange buttonhole and edging lace on waistcoat, gold hat lace. From 1736: grey-white lining and waistcoat, white gaiters.

Des Landes *or* Landes, incorporated into Hainault March 1749: Grey-white coat, cuffs, lining and breeches, red waistcoat and stockings, brass buttons, orange buttonhole lace on waistcoat, gold hat lace. From 1736: grey-white waistcoat, white gaiters.

Enghien: Grey-white coat, red cuffs (five buttons), lining, waistcoat, breeches and stockings, pewter buttons, silver hat lace, double vertical pockets, each with a button at the top and bottom and three at the centre. From

Languedoc Regiment, 1757. This uniform was also worn in Canada from late 1757. (Musée de l'Armée, Paris)

Soissonnois Regiment, 1757. Soldiers taking a nap, fully dressed, in what seems to have been the typical army tent – of white canvas with blue stripes and edging. (Musée de l'Armée, Paris)

Conti Regiment, 1757. Card playing was very popular among soldiers. Note the centre figure wearing his fatigue cap with the flap turned down. (Musée de l'Armée, Paris)

Berry Regiment, 1757. This uniform was also worn by the 2nd and 3rd battalions in Canada from 1757 to 1760. (Musée de l'Armée, Paris)

1736: grey-white lining, waistcoat and breeches, white gaiters. 1753: red collar and waistcoat. 1758: grey-white coat, lining and breeches, red collar, cuffs (five buttons) and waistcoat, pewter buttons, silver hat lace, double vertical pockets, each with five buttons.

Grenadiers de France: Formed on 10 February 1749 from the grenadiers of the regiments abolished after the war of Austrian Succession, the corps had four battalions of 12 companies, each of 45 men, augmented to 52 in December 1762. Disbanded August 1771. Blue coat and cuffs, red collar, lapels and lining, pewter buttons, white buttonhole lace ending in a point, blue waistcoat and breeches, black bearskin cap with red bag (hat with silver lace also worn). From 1763: blue coat, lemon yellow collar, cuffs, lapels (seven buttons each and four below) and lining, pewter buttons, white buttonhole lace, white waistcoat and breeches, bearskin cap with white metal plate and white cross on red back patch. From 1767: three buttons below the lapel, white lining, brass plate on cap.

Compagnies Franches: These few garrison independent companies were relics from earlier reigns and were posted in castles and forts. The Château du Taureau independent company was posted at Taureau castle in Brittany, and was disbanded around 1745. All grey-white uniform, double vertical pockets, brass buttons, gold hat lace and red cockade (Luynes' memoirs). The independent company under Captain Dreux then Captain Brezé in the 1740s was posted at the forts in the islands of St Marguerite and St Honorat, near Antibes in Provence. Disbanded in 1763. The Château de la Bastille and the Château de Vincennes independent companies were posted as garrisons in these famous castles until 1749. All three companies had grey-white coat, cuffs, waistcoat and breeches, red lining, brass buttons, gold hat lace. All these independent garrison companies were gradually replaced by invalid companies.

Invalides: The 'Invalids' had been instituted by Louis XIV in 1670 to care for officers and soldiers made infirm by wounds suffered on service. The magnificent *Hôtel Royal des Invalides* in Paris could contain up to 4,000 pensioners, many of whom were seriously crippled. There they found decent lodging and food and received medical care from nursing Sisters of Charity. There were many more invalids who were less 'infirm'. They were posted to forts and cities in the realm to perform light garrison duties. They were organised into 'detached' infantry companies, each of about 60 men. In 1758 there were some 135 companies plus four companies of artillerymen (posted at Toulon, Caen, Saint-Malo and Douay). The uniform for all invalids was a blue coat with red cuffs and lining, grey (later white) waistcoat, breeches and stockings, pewter buttons, plain hat. In 1767 the uniform was reported the same except that the coat had a small blue standing collar and that the pensioners lodged at the Invalides in Paris had blue waistcoat and breeches instead of white.

METROPOLITAN UNITS SENT OVERSEAS

Since the 1670s French colonial defence had been the prerogative of the Ministry of the Navy, which maintained garrisons of colonial troops in America, and of the *Compagnie des Indes* – the French East India Company – which posted its own colonial troops in Africa and Asia (see Vol. 5). No metropolitan troops from the Ministry of War were to serve overseas.

The first crack in this policy occurred in 1746, the year after the fall of Louisbourg (now in Nova Scotia, Canada). The government called upon the Ministry of War for reinforcements. Two battalions of the Ponthieu Regiment, a battalion of the Saumur royal militia and a battalion of the Fontenay-le-Comte royal militia were embarked on the fleet commanded by the Duke d'Anville which sailed to retake Louisbourg. At that time the Saumur royal militia battalion had the same uniform as the Poitou regular regiment, and Fontenay-le-Comte had that of the Touraine regular regiment. Plagued by misfortune and dispersed by a hurricane, the expedition failed utterly. However, the idea of using metropolitan army troops from the Ministry of War to reinforce the colonies in emergencies remained.

In 1755, apprehending war with Britain, the French court ordered again several battalions of *troupes de terre* to reinforce the colonial garrisons in New France. Thus, in spite of a British attempt to intercept them, the 2nd battalions of the regiments of La Reine, Languedoc, Béarn and Guyenne landed in Quebec City and the 2nd battalions of Artois and Bourgogne in Louisbourg.

The uniforms supplied in 1755 to the six battalions sent to New France were somewhat different from the standard regimental dress. These uniforms were issued after the battalions landed in New France, and were used from mid 1755 to about September 1757. They consisted of the standard grey-white coat, coat lining and breeches, but other details could differ significantly: La Reine had red cuffs and red waistcoat (rather than blue) with pewter buttons and false silver hat lace; Béarn had blue cuffs and blue waistcoat (instead of red) with pewter buttons and false silver hat lace; Guyenne had red cuffs and red waistcoat with brass buttons and false gold hat lace; and Languedoc had blue cuffs and blue waistcoat with brass buttons and false gold hat lace. None is listed as having coat collars. Artois had grey-white cuffs and grey-white waistcoat with brass buttons and false gold hat lace. Bourgogne had grey-white cuffs and grey-white waistcoat with pewter buttons and false silver hat lace.

Cambis Regiment, c.1758. The regimental colours had red (upper left and lower right) and green (upper right and lower left) quarters. Upon the surrender of the Fortress of Louisbourg, on 26 July 1758, the British refused the Honours of War to the French garrison which had bravely held out as long as possible with no hope of relief. Finding this most unfair, the men of Cambis' 2nd battalion burned their colours and broke their muskets rather than hand them over. (Fortress Louisbourg National Historic Site)

Piedmont, Normandie and La Marine regiments, 1760. Note the black lapels on Normandie's waistcoat. In this manuscript showing the infantry of France, presented to King Carlos III of Spain in 1760, the accoutrements are white with fusiliers carrying only bayonets. (Royal Library, Madrid)

Cambrésis, Tournaisis and Foix regiments, 1760. Uniforms were often almost identical from one regiment to the next. These three regiments all had grey-white with red cuffs and collar and brass buttons, but Cambrésis, which served in Mauritius between 1760 and 1764, had elaborate pocket flaps as distinctions; Foix, which served in Haiti from 1762 to 1765, had a blue waistcoat instead of red. (Royal Library, Madrid)

The button placement on these uniforms is unknown, but it could well have been that regimental tailors set them according to their unit's traditional dress. Forage caps were grey-white with the turnup in the regimental facing colour. White gaiters, shoes and black cravats were among the items issued to these battalions.

All drummers' uniforms sent in 1755 were of the king's livery of blue lined red with the small livery lace. This was fine for all units except La Reine, whose drummers had the queen's livery of red lined blue with the queen's livery lace. There is no information on how La Reine solved this problem but it must have been to the satisfaction of the proud officers and men of the queen's own regiment.

From the later part of 1757 the uniform of the six battalions sent to Canada and Louisbourg in 1755 became similar to their regiment in France.

The arms and equipment were the same as in France, but in Canada the swords of the fusiliers were ordered left in stores. However, grenadiers kept their sabres. Sergeants and officers also left their halberds and spontoons in store and were issued with muskets, bayonets and cartridge boxes.

In Canada (but not Louisbourg), officers and men were also issued extra equipment when campaigning in the wilderness. In the summer this consisted of a blanket, a capot (basically a blanket coat with a hood), a forage cap, two cotton shirts, a pair of breeches, a pair of drawers, a

Durfort, Provence and Cambis regiments, 1760. These grenadiers wear bearskin caps, small ventral cartridge boxes with a brass grenade on the flap, and a brass match case on the shoulder belt. (Royal Library, Madrid)

Grenadiers de France, Beauvoisis and Rouergue regiments, grenadiers, 1760. All have the distinctive bearskin caps, small ventral cartridge box and match case. (Royal Library, Madrid)

pair of '*mitasses*' (Indian-style leggings), a knife and a tomahawk. In winter additional equipment was issued. It consisted of pairs of moccasins, socks, mitts, a vest, thick *mitasses* of blanket cloth, pairs of deerskin shoes, a pair of snowshoes, a deerskin, a bearskin, a portage collar and two double-edged knives.

The 2nd battalions of La Sarre and Royal-Roussillon arrived in Quebec City with General Montcalm in 1756, and the 2nd and 3rd battalions of Berry in 1757. The 2nd battalion of Cambis and the 2nd battalion of *volontaires-étrangers* (see Vol. 3) reached Louisbourg just before the siege began, in 1758.

Army battalions were also sent to reinforce the French East India Company troops. The 1st and 2nd battalions of Lorraine arrived in India in 1757, followed by Lally's Irish Regiment (see Vol. 3) in 1758, but the remnants of both surrendered at Pondichery in January 1761. The Cambrésis Regiment left France in March 1760 for Île-de-France (Mauritius), where it remained in garrison until August 1763.

The fall of Guadeloupe in 1759 revealed to the French court the urgency of reinforcing the West Indian islands. Fifteen companies of royal grenadiers from the royal militia (see below) were posted in Martinique from August 1760, but the island nevertheless fell to British forces in January 1762. By then, a substantial force had sailed from France to reinforce its islands. It arrived too late to save Martinique and

Fifer, Piedmont Regiment, 1757-1760. Hat edged with white plumes and red, blue and white cockade, blue coat with red cuffs, wings and turnbacks, white and red lace and red waistcoat and breeches. (Watercolour by C. Becker, Weimar Library)

Piece of the king's small livery lace – a white chain on crimson background. (Private collection)

landed at Saint-Domingue (Haiti) in May 1762. The reinforcements consisted of a battalion each from the regiments of Boulonnois, Foix, Quercy and Royal-Barrois (see Vol. 3) and the Piquets de St Domingue (see below), who joined the local colonial troops, and the royal grenadiers, exchanged from Martinique.

The Piquets de Saint-Domingue was a temporary unit formed in July 1761 and sent to Saint-Domingue. It consisted of six piquets of 50 men each commanded by a captain and a lieutenant. It included 120 volunteers drawn from the Montmorency regiment, 30 from each of the 2nd battalions of the Languedoc, Guyenne, Béarn, Berry, La Reine and La Sarre regiments returned from Canada. Ordered amalgamated into other regiments in January 1763. Each piquet wore its own regiment's uniform and added a crimson collar, a yellow aiguillette and an epaulette of a distinctive colour.

For Louisiana, ten companies of the Angoumois regiment were posted in New Orleans from April 1762 to October 1763. For French Guyana, 100 men from the Bigorre Regiment arrived at Cayenne in July 1762. Some 650 men from La Marine, Montrevel, Beauvoisis and Penthièvre captured and held St John's, Newfoundland, from June 1762 until retaken by the British in September

Apart from the battalions sent to Quebec and Louisbourg in 1755, whose uniforms, worn until 1757, are described above, all units sent overseas wore the same uniform as in France.

POST-1762 REFORMS

From 20 December 1762 the whole army was shaken by Choiseul's sweeping reforms, which reduced the number of French infantry regiments from 88 to 66.

A profound change in French peacetime defence policy was assigning 23 regiments (40 battalions), nearly all of *infanterie française*, to serve as marines and in colonial garrisons on a rotating basis. But what worked well for the British was not so effective for the French. Martinique, Guadeloupe and adjacent islands in the West Indies and Île-de-France (Mauritius) and Île-de-Bourbon (La Réunion) in the Indian

LEFT **Private, Piedmont Regiment, 1757-1760.** Hat laced with false gold, white uniform with black collar and cuffs, brass buttons and buff accoutrements. (Watercolour by C. Becker, Weimar Library)

RIGHT ***Ein Frantzos*** **(a Frenchman) private of an unidentified line infantry regiment, 1757-1760.** Hat laced with false gold, white coat and turnbacks (no collar), blue cuffs, waistcoat and breeches, white buttons and narrow buttonholes, and buff accoutrements. (Watercolour by C. Becker, Weimar Library)

Ocean were selected for garrison by the metropolitan regiments. But many complaints, from the units who were not keen on overseas service and from the colonies who preferred to have their own colonial regiments, eventually brought about a cancellation of this policy. This happened first in the Indian Ocean from 1766, and then in Martinique and Guadeloupe from 1772.

The uniform of the *infanterie française* was transformed by the ordinance of 10 December 1762 and adopted from 1763. It had a tighter, more cut-away white coat, said to have been inspired by the Prussians. All regiments now had lapels, and all waistcoats were white. The buttons were henceforth stamped with the regimental number.

The facing colours of many regiments changed and were shown in various ways on the collar, cuffs and lapels. Many retained distinctive button arrangements on the pocket flaps and cuffs. These changes from 1762 to 1763 are far too numerous to list in this small volume, especially as there were further changes in 1767, when grenadier bearskin caps, which had been generally worn for years, finally became official head-dress. Fusiliers continued to wear tricorns, but there were many experiments with various sorts of helmets during the 1760s and early 1770s.

Officers were ordered to wear epaulettes which, for the first time, indicated not only the status of a regimental officer but also their rank. A colonel had two gold or silver epaulettes with bullion fringe, lieutenant-colonels one on the left shoulder, a major two epaulettes with strand fringe, a captain one on the left shoulder, a lieutenant one lace epaulette strap with silk diamonds and mixed gold or silver and silk fringes, and a sub-lieutenant one silk and lace epaulette and mixed fringes.

ABOVE **Private of an unidentified line infantry regiment, 1757-1760.** Hat laced with false gold, white coat and turnbacks (no collar), red cuffs, waistcoat and breeches, yellow buttons and narrow buttonholes and buff accoutrements. The caption erroneously says '*Ein Frantzos von Fischerschen Corps*', but Fischer's Corps was German and had green uniforms and facings. (Watercolour by C. Becker, Weimar Library)

Private and officer, Languedoc Regiment, 1761. The regiment's new blue lapels are shown but not the blue piping on the waistcoat on this German print by Raspe. (Anne S.K. Brown Military Collection, Brown University)

Régiments de Recrues

To implement the recruiting reforms of 1762/63 some 31 'regiments of recruits' were organised across the realm. This began in February 1763 and peaked at 33 regiments in 1765. This plan to institute centralised recruiting did not work very well, and in December 1766 a total of 26 regiments were disbanded, leaving only seven – then six from April 1767.

The remaining units were disbanded in May 1768, and recruiting was assumed by regiments. The infantry recruits of these regiments were issued a plain white coat, waistcoat and breeches, pewter buttons and white hat lace. Cavalry recruits had buff breeches and artillery recruits had red waistcoat and breeches. Sergeants' uniforms conformed to the above but had silver lace edging the cuffs. Officers had orange lapels (four buttons each), silver and orange epaulettes, silver buttons and hat lace. Drummers wore the king's livery with lace edging the cuffs only.

From 1767 infantry recruits had blue collar and lapels, brass buttons (three on the cuff, five per lapel and four below the right lapel), and silver hat lace. Cavalry recruits had blue coat, collar and cuffs, red lapels and lining, buff waistcoat and breeches, and brass buttons set as above.

Régiment des Recrues des Colonies

This was a recruits regiment of six companies, created on 30 April 1765 for the 23 army regiments posted in the colonies. It was posted at Île de Ré and sent recruits to the West Indies until it was disbanded in March 1773, following the recall of metropolitan army regiments from colonial garrisons. The uniform of cadres was white coat, waistcoat and breeches, green collar, cuffs and lapels, pewter buttons (six small under the cuff, five on each lapel, and three below the right lapel) and white hat lace. Recruits were each issued a waistcoat, a pair of breeches, a hat, a pair of black and a pair of white gaiters, shoes, stockings, a cravat, brushes and a hair powder bag.

Sappers, which had existed in various roles, officially came into the establishment in 1766/67. They were assigned an axe, a leather apron and a bearskin cap (without a plate and 3cm lower than a grenadier's).

MILITIA

Apart from its large regular army, France had a sizeable militia which was basically grouped into three types of organisations. The first, and largest, was the royal militia; the second the coast guard militia; and the third the bourgeois militia. The royal and coast guard militias were the country's territorial army reserves and were controlled by the government. They were considered part of the royal forces and listed as such in the army registers. Because it formed, in effect, the reserve of the *infanterie française*, the royal militia is included in this volume.

The coast guard militia evolved into largely an artillery corps, and will be covered with that arm in Vol. 3. The third type, the bourgeois militia, was not considered part of the army perse, but was mostly used for police as well as local military duties. This will be covered in Vol. 4. Colonial militias will be covered in Vol. 5.

Royal Militia

The royal or provincial militia was a draft system to conscript young men in France's 30,000 rural villages to form a reserve army. The regency of Louis XV had formed many militia units in 1719/20 but there was no permanent royal militia organisation in peacetime until 1726.

On 25 February 1726, as Europe seemed on the brink of a generalised conflict, the government decided to draft for garrison duty 60,000 militiamen between the ages of 16 and 40 led by 1,300 officers. They were organised into 100 battalions, each battalion divided into six companies of 100 men, later into 12 companies of 50 men each. A company of grenadiers was added to each battalion in 1734. The battalions were known by the name of the commanding lieutenant-colonels. When not in service, in war or peace, the militiamen lived in their villages or town, but they were always liable to be called up for

Fusilier, Boulonnois Regiment, 1776, wearing the helmet of neo-classical design which was tried in some infantry regiments during the 1760s and early 1770s. From 1763 the uniform was white with a green collar and pewter buttons. (Print after a contemporary painting)

Grenadier, La Reine Regiment, 1767. Bearskin cap with brass plate and white plume, white coat with crimson collar, cuffs and lapels, white turnbacks, white metal buttons, and white waistcoat, breeches and gaiters. (National Archives of Canada)

assemblies and reviews of their battalions over a four-year period. Service was raised to six years in 1734.

When war did come, in 1734/35, 122 battalions were mobilised for garrison duty. A few battalions from Franche-Comté, Languedoc and Provence were even in Germany and northern Italy. From the later 1730s the battalions were reduced to 100. From 1742 they assumed the geographical names of their provincial recruiting area and their precedence in the army was henceforth recorded. The city of Paris had not previously been included in the royal militia drafts but, from 1742 it was called upon to provide 1,800 men divided into three battalions.

On 10 April 1745 the battalions' grenadier companies were grouped into regiments of *grenadiers-royaux* (royal grenadiers) each of 12 companies of 50 men who soon distinguished themselves in battle. The proportion of militiamen came up to 32 per cent of the infantry during the war of Austrian Succession.

From 1756 the 112 royal militia battalions were used as a reserve to draft men into the regular line infantry regiments, while the royal grenadiers were deployed on various fronts. The proportion of militiamen was some 29 per cent of the army during the Seven Years War. They were sent home in 1763, but the royal militia was recalled in 1765 and transformed into 47 provincial regiments and 11 royal grenadier regiments. The Royal Grenadiers now had the names of provinces. The next year, Buttafuoco's Corsican Regiment (see Vol. 3) was converted into *Provincial de Corse*, and in 1773 six more provincial regiments and a 12th royal grenadier regiment were added.

From 1726 arms and accoutrements were supplied by the government but the uniform had to be paid for by the local provincial intendancy. As a result, the clothing was somewhat simple and plain. Privates and corporals each had a grey-white coat with grey-white cuffs, lining, waistcoat, breeches and stockings, pewter buttons, and false silver hat lace. Sergeants had the same but with blue cuffs and stockings and fine silver hat lace. The two Alsace battalions, however, had a distinctive blue and red uniform from the late 17th century. In 1735, for instance, Hannincq's battalion wore blue coats with red cuffs, waistcoats, breeches and stockings, pewter buttons, silver hat lace and bearskin caps for grenadiers.

In the later 1730s some or all battalions took to wearing the uniform of the line infantry regiment of their province. This practice was frowned upon, and in November 1746 the uniform was ordered to be completely grey-white with pewter buttons (four to each cuff and pocket) and silver hat lace. Sergeants now had grey-white cuffs edged with silver lace. This remained unchanged until after the Seven Years War.

From 1765 the royal militia's uniform was ordered to be white coat, lapels, lining, waistcoat and breeches, blue cuffs and collar, pewter buttons, and hat edged with white lace. It should be noted that the Paris battalions raised from 1742 also had an all grey-white uniform, but with brass buttons and false gold hat lace.

The royal grenadiers had the same uniform as the militia battalions but were distinguishable by blue and white epaulettes, although a blue collar and epaulettes of other colours seem to have been used during the Seven Years War. From 1765 their epaulettes were: Guyenne, blue; Poitou, red; Dauphiné, violet; Soissonnois, orange; Orléanois, green; Bretagne, black; Evéchés, blue and white; Lorraine, red and white;

Artois, yellow and white; Languedoc, red and black; and Bourgogne, green and white. The royal militia and royal grenadiers' drummers had blue coats with red cuffs and lining laced with the king's livery lace.

A few provinces had peculiar arrangements with the royal government, which allowed them to form their own militia units. Boulonnois had three regiments of 13 companies each, Navarre had one regiment of 24 companies, Béarn had a three-battalion regiment and Roussillon had five battalions. These troops served mostly as garrisons in forts, but also supplied recruits to the regular army. All were disbanded on 20 November 1762.

COLOURS

Each French line infantry regiment carried two types of colours: a colonel's colour and several 'ordonnance' colours, the French equivalent to the British king's colour and regimental colours. The colonel's colour was carried by the senior company of the first battalion.

There were two regimental colours in the first battalion and three for other battalions until February 1749, when the number was reduced to one in the first battalion and two in other battalions. They measured about 160cm square with crosses about 32cm wide and fixed to the pole with gilt nails. The pole had a gilt spear. Cords were in the colours of the flag.

French flags also had a white 'cravat', which was a narrow silk sash tied below the spear. Nearly all infantry colours had a white cross, with white quarters for the colonel's colour and the white cross with coloured quarters for the regimental colours. There were many variations, and some colours had quarters with very complicated designs. Most colours were plain, but some had lilies, badges and mottos painted on the silk.

LIVERIES FOR MUSICIANS

Drummers wore the livery of the 'owner' of the regiment. In most cases this meant the blue-lined-red livery coat of the king. The most senior regiments had 'grand' livery lace; the others had 'small' livery lace (see Vol. 1 MAA 296). The waistcoat and breeches would be as the men but red was often used also. Hats were sometimes seen with plume edging. Up to December 1762 many regiments belonged to noble 'gentlemen' whose name they bore and whose livery was worn by their drummers.

Drum belts and sword belts were usually edged or covered with livery lace. The drum cases were of the coat colour with the coat of arms

Officer, Du Roi Regiment, 1770. White uniform with blue collar, cuffs, lapels and turnbacks, gold buttons, epaulette and lace, black leather helmet with gilt furnishings, black mane and leopard-hide turban. (Print after contemporary painting)

painted in front, often surrounded by trophies. The drum hoops could be of the coat colour only, the lining colour or a combination of the livery colours. The liveries presently known for infantry regiments are:

Beauffremont: buff lined blue, silver lace. Boufflers: green lined red, white lace with small red 'molettes' and crosses, gold laces in between. Bourbon: yellow-buff lined red, red lace, silver laces in between and edging the cuffs. Brancas: 'damas' coloured coat (probably a shade of red) with yellow cuffs. Chartres: red lined blue, blue lace with white and red checked borders. Condé: yellow-buff lined red, red cuffs, red velvet lace. Conti: yellow-buff coat, blue cuffs, lining, waistcoat and breeches, silver hat lace. Cossé-Brissac: yellow lined black. Estaing: had permission to wear the same livery as the king. Luxembourg: buff lined blue, white or silver lace. Lyonnois: livery of Villeroi worn until c.1734: green lined aurore, aurore cuffs, aurore lace edged gold, white crosses edged gold with silver fleurs de lis on tips set on chest and back. Maine: red lined blue, yellow lace between two blue laces, boot cuffs and cross pockets. Monaco: red lined red, white or silver lace. Montmorency: buff lined blue, white or silver lace. Noailles: red. Penthièvre: red lined blue, yellow and blue lace. La Reine: red lined blue, blue lace with white chain. Rohan: red livery, green and white lace brandebourgs. Saint-Simon: yellow. Toulouse: red lined blue, yellow lace between two blue laces, slash cuffs and slash pockets. Vendôme: red lined blue, yellow lace between two blue lines, cross pockets.

Following the orders of 19 December 1762 drummers continued to wear the blue coat with the king's small livery lace, or the livery of the queen or the princes, but with the regimental facings. In the 1760s the drums gradually changed from wood to brass. In April 1766 a fifer and two clarinet players per battalion were added to the establishment, the nucleus of what was to become regimental bands. These musicians had a blue coat with a silver lace edging the cuffs but no livery lace.

SELECT BIBLIOGRAPHY

Boudriot, Jean, *Armes à Feu Françaises*, Modèles d'Ordonnance, Paris 1963

de Chennevières, *François, Détails Militaires...*, Paris 1750 (6 Vols)

Corvisier, André, *L'Armée Française de la Fin du XVIIe Siècle au Ministère de Choiseul: le Soldat*, Paris 1964 (2 Vols)

Kennet, Lee, *The French Armies in the Seven Years War*, Durham, N.C. 1967

Léonard, Émile, *L'Armée et ses Problèmes au XVIIIe Siècle*, Paris 1958

de Luynes, Duc, *Mémoires sur la Cour de Louis XV (1735-1758)*, Paris 1860-1865 (17 Vols)

Mention, Louis, *L'Armée de l'Ancien Régime de Louis XIV à la Révolution*, Paris c.1890

Pétard, Michel, *Équipements Militaires de 1600 à 1870*, 1984-1985 (Vols 1 and 2)

Reboul, Colonel, *La Vie au XVIIIe Siècle: l'Armée*, Paris 1931

Susane, Louis, *Histoire de l'Infanterie Française*, Paris 1874 (5 Vols)

THE PLATES

A: Gardes-Françaises (The French Guards), 1740s and 1750s
A1: Officer, full dress, 1740s and 1750s The officer's dress coat and waistcoat was almost covered with fine silver lace and embroidery.
A2: Officer, undress, 1740s and 1750s The officer's 'ordinary' duty uniform was more lavish than the dress uniforms of most armies – note the fine embroidered buttonholes.
A3: Private, 1740s and 1750s Even privates in the Gardes-Françaises had laced uniforms and accoutrements edged with white leather.
A4: Drummer, 1740s and 1750s The king's 'grand' livery was quite ornate. The drums were blue (the coat colour, as was the custom in the French army) and strewn with yellow or gold lilies.

B: Infantry, 1720s
B1: Tourville Regiment, sergeant The typical dress and armament of an infantry sergeant of the 1720s. Many regiments still had the older style of halberd, with the axe blade shown here. Halberds were to be 1.95m high.
B2: Du Roi Regiment, private This unit was the king's own regiment in the line infantry and it was distinguishable by the orange lace on the coat and waistcoat. The cockade, which varied in this regiment, was white and red at this time.
B3: Lyonnois Regiment, drummer Although a territorial regiment, Lyonnois was commanded until 1734 by successive generations of members of the Villeroi family. Their coat of arms is shown on the drum case. Exceptionally, Louis XIV had permitted the drummers to wear the family's green and orange livery trimmed with gold, rather than the royal livery. The crosses on the coat were used in a few units at this time.
B4: Dauphin Regiment, officers Shown wearing regimental uniforms, but with gold lace on the waistcoats and plumes on the hats. Field officers were often mounted while company officers were always to be on foot with their men. (All figures after c.1720 plates by Delaistre, Musée de l'Armée, Paris)

C: INFANTRY, POLISH SUCCESSION WAR, 1734-1735
C1: Bourbonnois Regiment, drummer The blue lined red king's livery was laced with elaborate 'grand' livery for this senior regiment. The royal arms were painted on the drum. Gudenus, the main source for this figure, shows the drum sticks fastened to the drum collar. The regiment served at the siege of Philipsburg, where Gudenus sketched one of its drummers. He gives them all cravats tied in 'butterfly' bows; no doubt this was the prevailing fashion at the time.
C2: Bretagne Regiment, private of grenadiers Only moustaches and sabres denoted grenadiers at this time since their uniform was the same as the rest of the men. The regiment served in Germany at the siege of Philipsburg and the battle of Klausen.
C3: Richelieu Regiment, sergeant The halberd head is of the new model, introduced at the beginning of the 18th century. The regiment was at the siege of Philipsburg, where it stormed some of the outer works.

C4: Royal-Roussillon Regiment, officer with colour and private The regimental colours of Royal-Roussillon were a white cross strewn with gold lilies with blue upper left canton, red upper right, brown lower left and green lower right. The regiment served with distinction against the Austro-Sardinian troops in north-western Italy in 1734/35.

D: INFANTRY, AUSTRIAN SUCCESSION WAR, 1740s
D1: Touraine Regiment, grenadier This grenadier's knapsack is of the bag type, and his equipment was a hatchet carried slung to the cartridge box belt. The regiment served at Dettingen in 1743 then in Flanders at the siege of Ypres and Tournai, at the battle of Fontenoy in 1745, the sieges of Audernade, Termonde, Ath, Namur, the battle of Lawfeld in 1747, the sieges of Berg-op-Zoom and, finally, at Maëstricht in 1748.
D3: Penthièvre Regiment, drummer This drummer is wearing the red livery of the duke of Penthièvre. His coat of arms was painted on the drum case. The regiment was part of the army that captured Prague in 1741. It was then in Germany at Dettingen in 1743, and went on to Flanders, where it fought in a number of battles, including Fontenoy.

Invalids, 1757. Left: an officer wears a blue coat with red cuffs and lining, buttonholes with narrow silver lace, silver buttons, white waistcoat and stockings, blue breeches, plain hat. Centre: this appears to be a private who is armed with a pike because he has only one arm. Right: this private is armed with a musket and bayonet. Both privates wear blue coats with red cuffs and lining, pewter buttons, grey-white waistcoat, breeches and stockings, and plain hats. (Musée de l'armee, Paris)

the 'French' infantry units to have bearskin caps and lapels on the coat. The regiment was deployed in Germany from 1757 to 1762, participating in the invasion of Hanover and several battles, including Minden.

E3: Cambis Regiment, sergeant This unit was one of the few that had both gold and silver buttons and hat lace. The 1757 manuscript shows red lapels for this regiment but it may have been an experimental issue limited to a few soldiers. The army registers and a document describing the uniform of the 2nd battalion sent to Louisbourg do not mention lapels. (Rochefort Archives, 1E, Vol. 158)

E4: Auvergne Regiment, officer with colour These distinctive violet facings were first used on the regimental colours at the beginning of the 17th century as a sign of mourning for King Henry IV; later they were used on the uniform. The regiment campaigned in Germany from 1757 to 1762 and was renowned for its gallantry in action. One of the most famous incidents of French military history occurred at Clostercamps on the night of 15-16 October 1760. An Anglo-Hanoverian force was approaching the French camp through woods under the cover of darkness when a chasseur picket of Auvergne spotted the movements. The captain, chevalier d'Assas, moved towards the unknown column at the head of his few men. He suddenly shouted: 'Shoot, chasseurs, it is the enemy!', and was then rushed and killed by enemy bayonets. Auvergne suffered heavy losses in the ensuing battle, but captured a cannon and a colour, and d'Assas was credited with having saved the French army by his sacrifice.

F: INFANTRY IN CANADA, 1755-1757

F1: La Reine Regiment, sergeant All four figures on this plate wear the special uniform supplied to the battalions that came to Canada in 1755. It was issued by the Ministry of the Navy, so the coats were replaced every two years instead of three as in the metropolitan army. The uniforms supplied for these 2nd battalions in Canada were different to those of the parent battalions in Europe. None had a collar, and La Reine had red waistcoats instead of blue. Sergeants came to Canada with halberds but were issued with muskets and bayonets shortly after landing. (Arch. Nationales, Colonies, C11A, Vol. 100)

F2: Languedoc Regiment, private This private is wearing a relaxed camp dress including a forage cap and comfortable moccasins. These were all issue items for undress and campaign in Canada.

F3: Guyenne Regiment, officer with regimental colour, a white cross with buff and green quarters The colours were carried in battle in Canada but were burned shortly before the surrender of Montreal rather than being handed over to the British. The latter, to their shame, refused the Honours of War to the valorous small French corps who had put up such a spirited resistance.

F4: Béarn Regiment, corporal This battalion had the most notable variation in uniform: its facings changed from red to blue, with pewter instead of brass buttons. Corporals had wool lace on the cuffs to distinguish rank.

G: INFANTRY IN LOUISIANA, THE WEST INDIES AND INDIA, 1758-1763

G1: Lorraine Regiment, grenadier, India, 1758-1761 This regiment saw much action, notably at the capture of Cuddelore in May 1758, the failed siege of Madras in 1759

Militiaman, Royal Militia, 1726. The dress was very plain but the men were well armed. (Bibliothèque Nationale, Paris)

D4: Penthièvre Regiment, officers with colour The regimental colours had gold anchors at the ends of the white cross, with green and buff quarters. Despite having anchors on its colours, the regiment had nothing to do with sea service. Nevertheless, its successive colonels, the dukes of Penthièvre, held the venal office of Admiral of France – hence the anchor badge.

E: INFANTRY, 1750S

E1: La Reine Regiment, drummer The queen's livery was the reverse of the king's, but the coat of arms painted on the drum was the same as the king's. Besides its 2nd battalion in Canada from 1755 to 1760, La Reine's 1st battalion was in various French garrisons until 1760; from then until the end of the war it campaigned in Germany.

E2: Grenadiers de France Regiment, private This elite unit, dressed in the blue and red of the royal livery, was the first of

and Pondichery, where the remnants of the unit surrendered in January 1761. Turnback ornaments became increasingly varied during this period, but simple diamonds, shown on this figure, were still common.

G2 and G3: Angoumois Regiment, privates and drummers, Louisiana, 1762-1763 This regiment sailed from France to New Orleans fully equipped with uniform coats, waistcoats, breeches, gaiters and tricorns – laced with false silver for the men and fine silver for sergeants (Arch. Guerre, A1, Vol. 3624). The *fleur de lis* on the fusilier's turnbacks are shown for 1762 and were gaining popularity throughout the army.

G4: Grenadiers Royaux, private, Martinique and Haiti, 1760-1763 The first 250 men reached Martinique in August 1760, followed by another 500 in March 1761 to reinforce the depleted colonial troops. The Grenadiers Royaux formed two thirds of the regulars in garrison when the British attacked in January 1762. Following the surrender of Martinique, the Grenadiers Royaux were sent to Haiti. (E. Rufz, *Études historiques et statistiques sur la population de la Martinique, 1850*, Vol. 1)

G5: Saint-Domingue Piquets, corporal, Haiti, 1761-1763 A corporal of the Montmorency Regiment, which furnished 120 of the 300 men of this unit, is shown in the regiment's uniform with the Piquets' distinctive crimson collar and yellow aiguillette. (Arch. Guerre, A1, Vol. 3624)

H: INFANTRY, LATER PART OF SEVEN YEARS WAR, 1760-1763

H1: Bresse Regiment, sergeant The regiment was posted on the Atlantic coast during the war, and helped repulse the British landing at St Cast in 1758. From the end of 1758 all sergeants in the army were issued muskets with bayonets, which at last replaced the halberd. In 1760, as some regiments looked for a new, sharper style, no doubt to raise sagging morale as the disastrous Seven Years War drew to an end, Bresse took to wearing yellow buttonholes and blue breeches.

H2: Vaubecourt Regiment, officer Not only has the uniform assumed new features such as lapels, but the officer's armament is now a light musket and bayonet instead of a spontoon. This officer has comfortable leather breeches and soft boots – commonly worn on campaign in place of the regulation cloth breeches and gaiters. The regiment saw much action in Germany during the war.

H3: Saint-Chaumond Regiment, grenadier From 1760 this regiment had lapels of crimson, its new facing colour and grey-white waistcoats. By this time fur caps for grenadiers were becoming widespread in the army. This regiment was part of Soubise's army which was crushed at Rossbach in 1757. It was later posted on the Atlantic coast.

H4: La Marine Regiment, private This private carries, besides his knapsack, the canvas tent, which is usually shown as white with blue stripes. The buttonholes were a new feature adopted in about 1760. A detachment of La Marine was part of the force that raided and held St John's, Newfoundland, in 1762.

Militiaman, Royal Militia, 1757. He wears the plain all grey-white uniform with pewter buttons of the militia infantry battalions and points sadly towards the distant native village from which he, and many others, were drafted. Desertion from these battalions was common in wartime, especially when the militiamen were incorporated into regular regiments. (Musée de l'Armée, Paris)

Notes sur les planches en couleur

Gardes-françaises, 1740 à 1759
A1: Officier, grande tenue, 1740 à 1759. Le manteau et le gilet de grande tenue des officiers étaient presque totalement recouverts de fin galon d'argent et de broderies. **A2:** Officier, petite tenue, 1740 à 1759. L'uniforme "ordinaire" des officiers était plus orné que la plupart des uniformes de grande tenue de la plupart des armées, avec notamment de belles boutonnières brodées. **A3:** Simple soldat, 1740 à 1759. Même les simples soldats des Gardes Françaises avaient un uniforme galonné et des équipements bordés d'une ganse de cuir blanc. **A4:** Tambour, 1740 à 1759. La "grande" livrée du roi illustrée était très richement décorée. Les tambours étaient bleus, la couleur coutumière du manteau dans l'armée française, et parsemés de lis jaunes ou dorés.

Infanterie, vers 1720
B1: Régiment de Tourville, Sergent. L'uniforme et les armes typiques d'un sergent d'infanterie vers 1720. De nombreux régiments avaient encore l'ancien modèle de hallebarde avec la lame de hache illustrée ici. **B2:** Régiment Du Roi, simple soldat. Cette unité était le régiment du roi dans l'infanterie. Il se distinguait par le galon orange du manteau et du gilet. **B3:** Régiment du Lyonnois, tambour. Ce régiment, le Lyonnois, fut commandé jusqu'en 1734 par les générations successives des membres de la famille Villeroi, dont le blason apparaît sur le tambour. **B4:** Régiment du Dauphin. Les officiers portent l'uniforme du régiment mais avec un galon doré sur le gilet et un panache sur le chapeau. Les officiers de campagne étaient souvent à cheval alors que les officiers de compagnie étaient toujours à pied avec leurs hommes (Tous les personnages s'inspirent des planches de Delaistre, c. 1720, Musée de l'Armée, Paris)

Infanterie, Guerre de la succession polonaise, 1734-1735
C1: Régiment du Bourbonnois, tambour. La livrée du roi, doublée de bleu, était ornée de riches galons pour ce régiment très ancien. Les armes royales étaient peintes sur le tambour. **C2:** Régiment de Bretagne, simple soldat des grenadiers. Seuls la moustache et le sabre différenciaient les grenadiers à cette époque. **C3:** Régiment de Richelieu, sergent. La tête de hallebarde est le nouveau modèle, introduit au début du XVIIIe siècle. **C4:** Régiment du Royal-Roussillon, officier avec étendard et simple soldat.

Infanterie, Guerre de la succession autrichienne, vers 1740
D1: Régiment de Touraine, grenadier. Mis à part sa paquetage a la forme d'un sac, l'équipement des grenadiers comprenait une hachette portée sur la ceinture de la cartouchière. **D2:** Régiment de Ponthieu, sergent. **D3:** Régiment de Penthièvre, avec la livrée rouge du duc de Penthièvre. Son blason était peint sur le tambour. **D4:** Régiment de Penthièvre, officiers avec étendard. Les étendards de ce régiment comportaient des ancres dorées aux extrémités de la croix blanche, avec des quarts verts et chamois.

Infanterie, vers 1750
E1: Régiment de la Reine, tambour. La livrée de la reine était l'inverse de celle du roi mais le blason peint sur le tambour était le même que celui du roi. **E2:** Régiment des Grenadiers de France, simple soldat. Cette unité d'élite, habillée dans la livrée royale bleu et rouge, était la première unité d'infanterie française à porter des bonnets à poil et des manteaux à revers. **E3:** Régiment de Cambis, sergent. Cette unité était l'une des rares à posséder des boutons or et argent et des galons sur le chapeau. **E4:** Régiment d'Auvergne, officier et étendard. Les revers violets bien particuliers furent utilisés pour la première fois sur l'étendard de ce régiment au début du XVIIe siècle en signe de deuil après la mort d'Henri IV puis furent utilisés ensuite sur les uniformes.

Infanterie au Canada, 1755-1757
F1: Régiment de la Reine, Sergent. Les quatre per représentés sur cette planche portent l'uniforme spécial fourni aux bataillons qui arrivèrent au Canada en 1755. **F2:** Régiment du Languedoc, simple soldat. Il porte un uniforme de camp avec le calot et les mocassins confortables qui étaient distribués avec la petite tenue et la tenue de campagne au Canada. **F3:** Régiment de Guyenne, officier avec étendard du régiment, une croix blanche avec des quarts chamois et et vert. **F4:** Régiment du Béarn, caporal. Ce bataillon présentait le changement le plus important : ses revers passèrent du rouge au bleu et ses boutons étaient en étain au lieu d'être en cuivre. Les caporaux portaient un galon de laine sur les manchettes pour indiquer leur rang. Infanterie en Louisiane, aux Antilles et en Inde, 1758-1763

Infanterie en Louisiane, aux Antilles et en Inde, 1758-1763
G1: Régiment de Lorraine, simple soldat, Inde, 1758-1761. L'ornement des revers devint de plus en plus varié à cette époque mais de simples losanges, comme ici, restaient courants. **G2:** Régiment d'Angoumois, simple soldat et tambour, Louisiane, 1762-1763. Les fleurs de lis sur les revers du fusilier illustrées dans les Ms de 1762 ont devenaient de plus en plus populaires dans toute l'armée. **G3:** Grenadiers Royaux, simple soldat, Martinique et Haïti, 1760-1763. **G4 :** Piquets de Saint-Domingue, caporal, Haiti, 1761-1763. Un caporal du Régiment de Montmorency, vêtu de l'uniforme du régiment avec le col pourpre et l'aiguillette jaune bien particuliers des Piquets. (Arch. Guerre, A1, Vol. 3624).

Infanterie, fin de la Guerre de Sept Ans, 1760-1763
H1: Régiment de Bresse, sergent. À partir de fin 1758, tous les sergents de l'armée reçurent un mousquet muni d'une baïonnette qui remplaçait enfin la hallebarde. **H2:** Régiment de Vaubecourt, officier. Il a maintenant une mousquet léger et une baïonnette au lieu d'un esponton, et porte une culotte de peau confortable et des bottes souples au lieu de la culotte de tissu et des guêtres imposées par le règlement. **H3:** Régiment de Saint-Chaumond, grenadier. À partir de 1760, ce régiment avait des revers pourpres, sa nouvelle couleur de revers, et un gilet gris clair. À cette époque, les calots de fourrure des grenadiers devenaient une mode très répandue dans l'armée. **H4:** Régiment de la Marine, fusilier. Ce simple soldat porte, en plus de son paquetage, une tente en tissu, généralement reproduite en blanc avec des rayures bleues. Les boutonnières étaient un élément nouveau adopté vers 1760.

Farbtafeln

Gardes-Françaises, 40er und 50er Jahre des 18. Jahrhunderts
A1: Offizier in Galauniform, 40er und 50er Jahre des 18. Jahrhunderts. Die Jacke und die Weste der Galauniform der Offiziere war fast ganz mit Silberlitze und kunstvoller Stickerei bedeckt. **A2:** Offizier in Ausgehuniform, 40er und 50er Jahre des 18. Jahrhunderts. Die 'normale' Dienstuniform der Offiziere war viel prunkvoller als die meisten Galauniformen anderer Armeen und wies bemerkenswert kunstvoll verzierte Knopflöcher auf. **A3:** Gefreiter, 40er und 50er Jahre des 18. Jahrhunderts. In den Gardes-Françaises hatten sogar Gefreite Uniformen mit Litze, und ihre Ausrüstung war mit weißem Leder eingefaßt. **A4:** Trommler, 40er und 50er Jahre des 18. Jahrhunderts. Die 'grand' Livree des Königs, die hier abgebildet ist, war recht prunkvoll. Die Trommeln waren blau, die Uniformfarbe, wie es in der französischen Armee Sitte war, und mit gelben beziehungsweise goldfarbenen Lilien übersät.

Infanterie, 20er Jahre des 18. Jahrhunderts
B1: Tourville Regiment, Feldwebel. Typische Uniform und Bewaffnung eines Infanterie-Feldwebels in den 20er Jahren des 18. Jahrhunderts. Viele Regimenter hatten noch die Hellebarde älteren Stils, deren Axtklinge auf dieser Farbtafel abgebildet ist. **B2:** Du Roi Regiment, Gefreiter. Bei dieser Einheit handelte es sich um das Regiment des Königs in der Linieninfanterie, erkenntlich durch die orangefarbene Litze auf dem Waffenrock und der Weste. **B3:** Lyonnois Regiment, Trommler. Das Lyonnois-Regiment unterstand bis 1734 dem Befehl aufeinanderfolgender Generationen der Familie Villeroi, deren Wappen auf der Trommel abgebildet ist. **B4:** Offiziere des Dauphin Regiment trugen die Regimentsuniform, hatten jedoch Goldlitzen auf der Weste und Federbüsche auf der Mütze. Feldoffiziere waren oft zu Pferde, während Kompanieoffiziere stets mit ihren Männern zu Fuß gingen. (Alle Figuren beruhen auf Tafeln von Delaistre, ca. 1720, Musée de L'Armée, Paris).

Infanterie, polnischer Erbfolgekrieg, 1734-1735
C1: Bourbonnois Regiment, Trommler. Die blaugefütterte, rote Livree des Königs wies bei diesem dienstälteren Regiment Elemente der 'grand' Livree auf. Das königliche Wappen war auf die Trommel gemalt. **C2:** Bretagne Regiment, Gefreiter der Grenadiere. Grenadiere waren zu dieser Zeit lediglich durch ihren Schnurrbart und den Säbel erkenntlich. **C3:** Richelieu Regiment, Feldwebel. Die Spitze der Hellebarde entspricht dem neuen Modell, das zu Beginn des 18. Jahrhunderts eingeführt wurde. **C4:** Royal-Roussillon Regiment, Offizier mit Fahne und Gefreiter.

Infanterie, österreichischer Erbfolgekrieg, 40er Jahre des 18. Jahrhunderts
D1: Touraine Regiment, Grenadier. Sein Rucksack ist wie eine Reisetasche geformt, und zur Ausrüstung der Grenadiere gehörte ein Kriegsbeil, das am Patronentaschenriemen festgemacht war. **D2:** Ponthieu Regiment, Feldwebel. **D3:** Penthièvre Regiment, Trommler in der roten Livree des Herzogs von Penthièvre, dessen Wappen auf der Trommel auftaucht. **D4:** Penthièvre Regiment, Offiziere mit Fahne. Die Regimentsfahne wies an den Spitzen des weißen Kreuzes goldene Anker sowie grüne und gelbbraune Viertel auf.

Infanterie, 50er Jahre des 18. Jahrhunderts
E1: La Reine Regiment, Trommler. Die Livree der Königin stellte eine Umkehrung der des Königs dar, das Wappen auf der Trommel war allerdings das gleiche wie das des Königs. **E2:** Grenadiers de France Regiment, Gefreiter. Diese Eliteeinheit, im Blau und Rot der königlichen Livree gekleidet, war die erste der 'französischen' Infanterieeinheiten mit Bärenfellmützen und Revers auf der Jacke. **E3:** Cambis Regiment, Feldwebel. Diese Einheit gehörte zu den wenigen, die sowohl Gold- und Silberknöpfe als auch Mützenlitzen hatten. **E4:** Auvergne Regiment, Offizier mit Fahne. Die charakteristischen violettfarbenen Besätze tauchten erstmals Anfang des 17. Jahrhunderts als Zeichen der Trauer um König Heinrich IV. auf den Regimentsfahnen auf und wurden später auch auf der Uniform verwendet.

Infanterie in Kanada, 1755-1757
F1: La Reine Regiment, Feldwebel. Alle vier auf dieser Farbtafel abgebildeten Figuren tragen die spezielle Uniform, die an die Bataillone ausgegeben wurden, die 1755 nach Kanada kamen. **F2:** Languedoc Regiment, Gefreiter in einem ungezwungeneren Feldanzug mit Feldmütze und bequemen Mokkasins, alles Kleidungsstücke, die für Ausgeh- und Felduniformen in Kanada ausgegeben wurden. **F3:** Guyenne Regiment, Offizier mit Regimentsfahne in einem weißen Kreuz mit gelbbraunen und grünen Vierteln. **F4:** Béarn Regiment, Obergefreiter. Bei diesem Bataillon zeigten sich die auffälligsten Veränderungen, die Besätze waren nun nämlich blau statt rot und an die Stelle der Messingknöpfe traten Zinnknöpfe. Obergefreite hatten als Rangabzeichen Litzen aus Wolle an den Manschetten.

Infanterie in Louisiana, auf den Westindischen Inseln und in Indien, 1758-1763
G1: Lorraine Regiment, Gefreiter, Indien, 1758-1761. In dieser Epoche wurden die Verzierungen auf Aufschlägen immer vielseitiger, doch waren einfache Rhomben - wie bei der abgebildeten Figur - nach wie vor gang und gäbe. **G2:** Angoumois Regiment, Gefreiter und Trommler, Louisiana, 1762-1763. Die bourbonische Lilie auf den Aufschlägen des Füsiliers taucht in den 1762er Modellen auf und erfreute sich zunehmend großer Beliebtheit im ganzen Heer. **G3:** Grenadiers Royaux, Gefreiter, Martinique und Haiti, 1760-1763. **G4:** Saint-Domingue Piquets, Obergefreiter, Haiti, 1761-1763. Ein Obergefreiter des Montmorency Regiment in der Regimentsuniform mit dem charakteristischen purpurroten Kragen und der gelben Achselschnur der Piquets. (Arch. Guerre, A1, Vol. 3624)

Infanterie gegen Ende des Siebenjährigen Krieges, 1760-1763
H1: Bresse Regiment, Feldwebel. Ab Ende des Jahres 1758 wurden an alle Feldwebel der Armee Musketen mit Bajonetten ausgegeben, die endlich die Hellebarde ersetzten. **H2:** Vaubecourt Regiment, Offizier. Inzwischen hat er eine leichte Muskete und ein Bajonett anstelle einer Pike, er trägt bequeme Breeches aus Leder und weiche Stiefel anstelle der vorschriftsmäßigen Tuch-Breeches und Gamaschen. **H3:** Saint-Chaumond, Grenadier. Ab 1760 hatte dieses Regiment Revers in purpurrot, der neuen Besatzfarbe, und grauweiße Westen. Zu dieser Zeit kamen bei den Grenadieren weitgehend Pelzmützen in Mode. **H4:** La Marine Regiment, Füsilier. Abgesehen von seinem Rucksack trägt dieser Gefreite das Segeltuchzelt bei sich, das normalerweise als weiß mit blauen Streifen abgebildet ist. Die Knopflöcher waren ein neues Merkmal, das etwa um 1760 eingeführt wurde.